LOST CALIFORNIA TREASURE

T0274803

W. CRAIG GAINES

THE
History
PRESS

Published by The History Press
Charleston, SC
www.historypress.com

First published 2023

Manufactured in the United States

ISBN 9781467153614

Library of Congress Control Number: 2022950062

CONTENTS

PREFACE

This work is derived mostly from my collection of lost treasure and treasure hunting information, which began when I was in junior high school. I lived a few decades in California, roaming up and down the Central Valley, visiting the Mother Lode Country and traversing along the Coastal Range and Pacific Coast. I traveled El Camino Real, which connected the Spanish missions. These old missions were the birthplace of many lost treasure and lost mine stories.

Spanish Manila treasure galleons from the Philippines often wrecked on the California coast. Sir Francis Drake and his pirates were thought to have hidden plundered Spanish treasure along the Northern California coast. Spanish missions, pueblos and presidios eventually were established along the California coastal areas. During the period of colonial revolution, a pirating expedition along the California coast caused a number of treasures to be cached. Most of the missions have stories of lost padre mines in the Coastal Range that were abandoned when Mexico broke free of being a Spanish colony. Mexico expelled the padres and took over the missions in 1833. More tales of hidden padre treasure came from that time.

The influx of emigrants led to a number of lost treasures, especially among the ill-fated Donner Party, which became trapped in the Sierras during the winter of 1846–47. The American invasion of California during the Mexican-American War caused a number of treasures to be hidden from the invaders.

The discovery of gold at Sutter's Mill at Coloma in 1848 and the great gold rush that followed resulted in hundreds of millions of dollars in gold being mined from the Mother Lode, one of the richest concentrations of gold on Earth. It was odd that the Spanish never discovered gold in the Sierra Nevada Mountains, but they mostly settled the coast.

California has a huge number of lost mine stories. Most are from the early gold rush period. Many of these lost mines concern lost placer gold deposits or rich diggings that I believe were likely found and mined out since the 1850s. Others concern lost ledges or hard rock gold deposits that may indeed be lost, as they might have been small, rich deposits. A few lost mines were excuses for someone to finance some prospectors looking for minerals.

With the influx of prospectors and would-be miners came various undesirables who separated successful miners from their gold. Gamblers and robbers flooded the country looking for easy pickings. Gangs led by Joaquin Murieta (or Murrieta), Tom Bell and Tiburcio Vásquez robbed stagecoaches, stores and wary travelers. Stagecoach robberies and claim jumping were commonplace. The miners normally hid their gold in or near their shack or mining claim, as there were no local banks. A number of these caches of gold nuggets and gold dust along with gold coins are likely still hidden.

Many gold rush shipwrecks contained gold cargoes and gold carried by passengers. One of the shipwrecks, the *Brother Jonathan*, which sank in 1865, was partially salvaged in the 1990s. More than 1,500 shipwrecks are located around California and its offshore waters.

There are often multiple versions of many of the more famous lost mines and treasures. I sorted through these tales to present a logical sequence of events and indicated some variations in information in parenthesis. The locations of lost mines and treasure are often vague and different depending on the story version. If everyone knew the exact location of the lost treasure or mine, someone would have found it by now.

The stated value of lost treasures often seems too large for the times. Gold from the 1850s through the 1970s was worth only a fraction of what it is worth today. Nonetheless, California is called the Golden State for its huge amounts of gold mined and lost and still waiting to be discovered.

CALIFORNIA TREASURES
BY COUNTY

ALAMEDA COUNTY

ADAMS POINT TREASURE

In about 1893, two outlaws supposedly buried loot near the Lake Merritt tidal lagoon in Oakland in the Adams Point area. One outlaw killed the other over sharing the loot. The murdered outlaw's corpse was hidden near a brick oven. The surviving outlaw was soon captured by the law and sent to San Quinton Prison. Prior to dying in prison, he revealed the loot's location, but no one found it. Another version has the events taking place in 1895 with a search for $80,000 in gold coins in Oakland.

HIGUERA RANCH TREASURE

Near Rancho de los Tularcitios, $80,000 in gold coins was reportedly buried.

MURIETTA BRUSHY PARK CACHE

Bandit Joaquin Murietta reportedly had a hideout (cave) near Brushy Peak, about eight miles northeast of Livermore. Some suspected that he buried a cache nearby.

Alpine County

Ebbetts Pass Holdup Loot
Two stagecoach robberies occurred near the gold rush camp of Hangtown (now Placerville), with both gangs caching their loot in two different locations on the west side of the mountains before being killed or captured. Near Ebbetts Pass and present US-50, $22,000 in gold was supposedly hid. One site could be about fourteen miles above Placerville at a bend in a mountain road coming from Virginia City, Nevada. One story was that each gang thought the other gang was a posse after them, so they both cached their loot. These could be located in El Dorado County.

Lost Snowshoe Thompson Gold Mine
John A. "Snowshoe" Thompson was born in Norway on April 30, 1827, as Jon Torsteinson-Rue. In 1837, "Snowshoe" Thompson and his family moved to the United States from Telemarken, Norway. They lived in Illinois, Missouri, Iowa and Wisconsin. In 1851, Thompson drove cows to California, where he mined gold near Placerville (Hangtown), Kelsey Diggings, Coon Hollow and Georgetown. He worked in the Sutter Creek area and bought a ranch on Putah Creek and then a ranch in Diamond Valley. Thompson lived in Diamond Valley on 160 acres on the West Fork of the Carson River, between Fredericksburg and Woodfords. His ranch was about five miles west of the Carson Valley near Markleeville.

California gold miners sent letters home with bank drafts or money and received letters from their families in the East. During winter, snow closed the roads over the Sierra Nevada Mountains. Twice a month, Thompson carried mail from Placerville to as far as Carson City (Mormon Station), Nevada, and then back to Placerville for a fee. The mail he carried would then go by stagecoach to St. Louis, Missouri, to be distributed throughout the United States. Thompson made the narrow wooden skis he used to carry about one hundred pounds of mail each way in his backpack. Many called his skis "snowshoes."

On one of his many trips over the Sierra Nevada Mountains, Thompson halted on a ridge and looked down at his Diamond Valley home. He noticed white rock containing gold in an outcrop on the ground and picked up ore samples. This was possibly between Horseshoe Canyon and Hawkins Peak. He retrieved additional ore samples and later planned to eventually mine there. He told his wife about the gold ore.

Over the years, Thompson saved the lives of many people in the snow-covered Sierra Nevada Mountains. One of them, Jim (James) Sisson, left Placerville in the winter of 1859 with two mules carrying supplies and 420 pounds of gold nuggets. Sisson camped near Emerald Bay on Lake Tahoe. When he woke up, Sisson discovered that both of his legs had frozen solid. Thompson encountered Sisson and urged him to leave his gold behind and ride a mule out to get help. Thompson supposedly dug a shallow hole in the frozen ground and buried the gold nuggets.

There is another story that Jim Sisson had been alone in an unheated cabin for twelve days when Thompson discovered him. Thompson got a rescue party and returned with mules that carried Sisson to Carson City, Nevada. Jim Sisson could have stashed his gold nuggets, or maybe actually took the gold with him under this variation of the tale.

To save Jim Sisson's life, Dr. Deyton would have to amputate Sisson's legs, but he required chloroform. Thompson went over the Sierra Nevada Mountains, got the chloroform in Sacramento and returned to Carson City. Sisson recovered from his operation and reportedly told Thompson to get the

Snowshoe Thompson Memorial in Auburn. Thompson had a lost mine in the Sierra Nevada Mountains. He also has a lost gold story cache. *Author's collection.*

cached gold nuggets as a reward. Jim Sisson got on a stage and supposedly returned home without his gold. Thompson reportedly never recovered Sisson's gold nugget cache, which was on a trail near Echo Summit and Stateline, Nevada, probably not far from U.S. Highway 50.

In 1866, Snowshoe Thompson married Agnes Singleton. Thompson was on the Alpine County Board of Supervisors from 1868 to 1872 and a Republican State Convention delegate in Sacramento in 1871. The only money Thompson received for carrying mail over the mountains were small payments recipients sometimes paid.

Thompson carried mail over the Sierra Nevada Mountains from 1856 to May 15, 1876, when he got appendicitis and pneumonia and died. He was buried at the Genoa Cemetery. He reportedly never showed anyone where his rich gold ore came from or where Sisson's gold nuggets were hidden. Snowshoe Thompson's wife told others about his lost mine. She relayed how her husband said he could see the gold deposit's location from their Diamond Valley ranch.

LOST SONORA PASS LEDGE
See Mono County.

AMADOR COUNTY

JOE WILLIAMS TREASURE
Joe Williams reportedly cached $80,000 in gold coins in small wooden boxes buried no more than four feet apart near Drytown on Dry Creek. He had traded nuggets from his claim on Murderer's Gulch for the gold coins. From his deathbed, Joe Williams supposedly claimed, "Nobody will find it in a hundred years." Indeed, no one is known to have found it.

LOST RANCHERIA CREEK MINE
During the early gold rush, two miners were said to have worked a mine on Rancheria Creek near Drytown. The partners decided to return home to Pennsylvania with their gold and then later come back to their California claim. They concealed their mine and left California. One partner died, and the other partner became too ill to return to California until the 1890s. By then, mining and settlements had altered his markers to the mine.

Placer mining at the mining town of Volcano. Mining towns were often built on gold-bearing gravel and may have hidden miners' caches. *New York Public Library.*

His memory also failed him, so he did not locate his mine and finally left California for good.

SPANISH MINER'S CACHE
A Spanish miner may have cached $34,000 in gold nuggets in the 1870s near his cabin north of Fiddletown. The miner had been quite successful. He made loans in gold nuggets and gold coins to many people. In 1887, the Spanish miner died of a stroke. His hidden gold was said to have not been recovered.

THE LOST STRIKE
On Dry Creek, west of the mining town of Volcano, a Mexican miner had a gold claim. Upon hearing of another, more valuable strike, he hid his mine and left. The gold rush he left for did not pan out. When he returned to the area, he couldn't find his gold mine's location.

TOM BELL JACKSON LOOT
Near Pardee Reservoir, southwest of Jackson, outlaw Tom Bell reportedly cached loot. Bell had a hideout west of the present Pardee Reservoir and made several robberies north of Jackson City.

BUTTE COUNTY

BIDWELL'S LOST GOLD SHIPMENT

Rich entrepreneur General John Bidwell of Rancho Chico (Chico) owned many gold mines and much land. One of his gold shipments from the American River and Big Butte Creek was heading to Princeton Landing on the Sacramento River when Maidu Indians reportedly killed some of the drivers and captured the wagons. The attack possibly took place at a ford on Big Chico Creek a mile from Bidwell's headquarters. The Indians hid the strongbox of gold in a tree trunk before a posse caught up with them. Most of the Indians were immediately killed, and the surviving Indians were hanged after they told the story of hiding the strongbox. All the trees in the area eventually were cut down and many holes were dug, but no one reported finding the strongbox of gold. This could be located in Tehama County.

BUTTE CREEK TREASURE

A Wells Fargo and Company stage was robbed by four bandits near Butte Creek and Lowry's Ranch in about 1860. The stagecoach was forced to stop by a rope hung across the road where it crossed a dry slough. The robbers stole the strongbox with $16,000 in gold from the stagecoach. Bandit Oliver Grey was captured and sentenced to San Quentin for ten years. Bandit Frank Smith was arrested in Marysville and imprisoned for ten years. Some think that the robbers buried the treasure near Marysville or Butte Creek and never recovered it.

LOST HUMMINGBIRD MINE

This is said to be located near Butte Creek.

LOST NATIVE AMERICAN MINE

In 1884, an Indian arrived in Oroville with a bag of nuggets. He claimed that his mine could make fifty men rich for life. Prospectors tried to follow the Indian to the mine, but he always evaded them. On one of his trips to Oroville, the Indian became ill and died. The mining town of Cherokee is not far from Oroville, so the Indian could have been one of the Cherokees who had come to California during the gold rush.

ROBBERS TROVE

At Long Bar on the Feather River near Oroville, an outlaw gang robbed the Bentz & Company store. The outlaws stole three silver watches, two

Above: California gold mining methods in 1871. *Library of Congress.*

Left, top: A building ruin in the mining town of Cherokee, where Cherokee Indians mined gold. Several lost treasures may be located in this area. *Author's collection.*

Left, bottom: The North Fork of the Feather River was one of many Mother Lode rivers containing gold that have tales of lost gold mines. *Author's collection.*

gold breast pins, a large ring, several hundred dollars' worth of mercury, $500 in $10 and $20 gold coins, gold specimens and gold dust worth several hundred dollars in buckskin bags marked "Bentz and Company." The *Marysville Appeal* newspaper on September 28, 1853, ran an ad from Bentz & Company offering $500 for recovery of the stolen goods.

Posses searched between Long Bar and Marysville. Some thought that the loot was cached north of East Biggs or Rio Bonito. At a ford on the Gernadez Grant on the Feather River about fifteen miles north of Marysville, one posse composed of miners encountered two mysterious men about dark, four days after the robbery. The posse saw a burning cabin and stopped looking for the two men, as they went to help put out the fire and save the cabin occupant's possessions in what is now East Biggs. Fires in the Sierra are notorious for burning thousands of acres, so preventing a cabin fire from spreading was always critical. Some speculated that the cabin fire was started to help the outlaws escape the posse.

In 1909, farmer Henry Haselbusch found ten- and twenty-dollar gold pieces dated 1852 in the mud of a freshly plowed field after flooding that year. He and others searched the field but found nothing else. This was long before metal detectors were available. Some think that the coins were washed by floods from the cache's original burial place and that it was part of the loot from the Bentz & Company store robbery.

Three Finger Jack and Joaquin Murietta Treasure
A few miles south of Paradise, the infamous outlaws Three Finger Jack and Joaquin Murietta supposedly cached about 250 pounds of gold nuggets ($140,000) from a strongbox on a Feather River bank a few miles south of Paradise. Today, that amount of gold would be worth more than $6 million.

Calaveras County

Buster's Lost Gold
During the gold rush, an African American man named Buster discovered a rich gold deposit in the early 1850s at Mokelumne Hill. After much mining, he took the gold to Cueno's General Store. It was 136 pounds of gold ($220,000 in gold nuggets), which would be about $4 million in today's value. He built a cabin at the site of his gold claim on Buster's Gulch near San Antone Camp (Calaveritas) on San Antone Creek, a branch of the South

Fork of the Calaveras River. Buster reportedly hid gold in a Dutch oven near his cabin. Buster died in 1863 (another source claimed 1872). After Buster's death, miners tore down Buster's cabin and mined the cabin site to try to find Buster's gold cache. Charlie Vickers had taken care of Buster during his fatal illness. After Buster's death, Vickers seemed more affluent, so he may have gotten Buster's gold. Along the creek, a boy discovered an old empty Dutch oven, causing some to believe that Buster's gold had been recovered.

CAMP SECO GOLD CACHE
A southerner brought his slave Jim to Camp Seco before the Civil War. When his former master died, Jim inherited the mine and cabin in a draw of the Mokelumne River. Before Jim died, he claimed that several cans (jars and boxes) containing his former master's gold were buried near his cabin. Jim reportedly never found them.

DORRINGTON HOTEL CACHE
The Dorrington Hotel in Dorrington was said to be haunted by the ghost of Rebecca Dorrington Gardner, wife of John Gardner. During a storm, she went to check on her money cache near her barn or to deposit more cash there. She caught pneumonia and died. Her money was rumored to still be unfound.

INDIAN CEREMONIAL RIDGE GOLD
Not far from Murphys on Ceremonial Ridge, an Indian supposedly cached goose and turkey feather quills containing gold dust and nuggets. Other versions of the story claimed that gold artifacts, gold coins and silver coins were also buried in graves.

JACKASS HILL CACHE
Near Jackass Hill and Robinson's Ferry, about $15,000 in gold coins were said to have been cached.

LOST DOUGLAS FLAT GOLD LEDGE
While walking to Douglas Flat, a worker at Sheep Ranch supposedly stumbled across a rich gold ledge. After taking a few samples, he continued to his destination. When he tried to relocate the ledge, he was unable to find it. Reportedly, he paid $100 to a prospector to help him relocate the ledge, but they never found it.

Lost Golden Caverns Mine
This lost mine was said to have been near Columbia at the lower part of French Gulch.

Lost Gun Mine
In the Blue Mountains area, a prospector encountered a rich gold ledge when hunting. He broke his rifle prying a sample of the gold ore from the ledge. To mark the ledge, he left his rifle there, but he never was able to relocate it.

Lost Volcano Lake of Gold
Inside a dormant volcano, a mountain lake was reportedly found with gold scattered along its shore. This was said to be in the Feather and Yuba Rivers drainage basin, possibly between Lake Almador and the Sacramento River Valley. See Siskayou County and Shasta County for similar lost lakes of gold.

Lost Red Hankerchief Mine
While hunting, a man found some gold ore float on the bank of the Stanislaus River near Big Trees. He followed the float gold ore up to a ledge above the river and tied his red handkerchief to a tree limb to mark the find. After reporting this find to his partner and how he marked it with his red handkerchief, the hunter died in an accident.

Lost Sheep Ranch Gold Mine
This mine was rumored to be near Murphys.

Lost Sonoran's Treasure
A Mexican miner from Sonora supposedly buried $15,000 near his cabin in the mining camp called Whisky Slide northeast of San Andreas. An outlaw murdered the miner when he resisted his attacker after refusing to disclose his treasure's location.

Miner's Angels Camp Cache
William Miner was said to have cached $2,500 about three miles west of Angels Camp.

Angels Camp in the Mother Lode was a rich mining town. *Library of Congress.*

MOKELUMNE HILL CHINESE CACHE
A Chinese merchant reportedly buried his life savings in a strongbox near his Mokelumne Hill store.

MURIETTA SAN ANDRES CACHE
Bandit Joaquin Murietta and his gang were said to have cached loot near San Andres. One area mentioned is in the Calaveras forest region on the road between California Highway 49 and California Highway 88, between Angels Camp and Pioneer.

OLD HAWKINS CACHE
A cache of rich gold ore was reportedly near Hawkins Bar and old Hawkins.

PERALTA MINE
The Peralta family in Mexico were miners who had an Arizona mine associated with the Lost Dutchman Mine. Members of the Peralta family reportedly found a Sierra Nevada Mountains mine and sent gold nuggets back to Mexico. Several locations were given for its site, including near Angels Camp or Jenny Lind up the Calaveras River or about twelve miles below Lake Almanor in Plumas County.

Colusa County

Sterling's Gold

In the 1850s, Charles Sterling was a successful prospector who reportedly buried over $25,000 in gold dust in liquor bottles on a slough at French Crossing on Butte Creek. Upon his death, no one knew where he cached his gold.

The *Belle*'s Treasure

The steamer *Belle* left Sacramento for Red Bluff up the Sacramento River. Near Grimes, the *Belle*'s boiler blew up on February 5, 1856, killing most of its sixty passengers and crew. Two express men, Robert McCabe (of Rhodes & Company) and Charles Bowen (of Wells Fargo), reportedly had $100,000 in gold in a safe on the *Belle*. Other treasure and dry goods owned by Wines and Company and Pacific Company Expresses were reportedly salvaged. The remains of the ship were towed to shore. A monument to clerk Leonidas Taylor, whose body was never found, is on the road on the levee at the site of the disaster. Much work has been done on this area of the Sacramento River channel over the years.

Contra Costa County

Dr. Marsh's Lost Fortune

Rich doctor and Sacramento Delta landowner Dr. John Marsh hid his fortune. Some claimed that it was as much as $435,000 (or $50,000). Marsh controlled seventeen thousand acres between Mount Shasta and the San Joaquin River, which he later expanded to more than fifty thousand acres. His empire consisted of trading, ranching, farming and gold mining. Between his ranch and Martinez, he was seized by robbers, tortured and murdered on September 24, 1856. Another version of his death was that he had a money dispute with some employees who killed him. His fortune could be hidden on Rancho Los Melganos in the Brentwood area. Marsh's ranch house was called the Stone House.

Mount Diablo Gold

In about 1776, as Mission San Francisco de Asis was constructed, Indians supposedly brought gold nuggets from what they said was Mount Diablo

Several treasure caches are in the Sacramento River Delta islands. *Author's collection*.

Mount Diablo towers above the Central Valley. It has a lost gold mine legend associated with it. *National Archives*.

(Devil's Mountain). The padres feared that the discovery of gold would disrupt their new mission. According to this tale, the padres secretly coated the gold nuggets with poison. The padres put the poison-laced gold in a tub of water. When the Indians' dogs drank the water, the dogs died. The padres claimed that the gold was poison and evil. Thereafter, these Indians avoided gold and talking about it. Searches for a lost gold mine on Mount Diablo have not found gold, but mined cinnabar (mercury) used in gold extraction from ore was mined on Mount Diablo along with coal. Mount Diablo is located just east of Walnut Creek; it is 3,849 feet high and towers over this part of the Central Valley. Mount Diablo State Park covers the area now. It's likely that any gold nuggets associated with this story actually came from the Sierra Nevada Mountains and that the padres misunderstood what the Indians were trying to tell them.

RED ROCK TREASURE

South of Richmond, near the east end of the Richmond–San Rafael Toll Bridge, which crosses San Pablo Bay, is the island of Red Rock. Red Rock was originally called Treasure Rock or Golden Rock, after a Spanish treasure that was reportedly cached there.

DEL NORTE COUNTY

BROTHER JONATHAN TREASURES

The 1,359-ton wooden sidewheel steamer Brother Jonathan (formerly Commodore) was constructed in 1851 in New York City. It had a 220-foot length and a 36-foot beam. The California Steam Navigation Company–owned Brother Jonathan was transporting 120 cabin passengers, 72 steerage passengers and 50 officers and crew on its voyage north. Among its cargo were 346 barrels of whiskey, 100 tons of machinery for the Providence Mining Company, mill equipment, $10,000 (or $25,000 in gold coins) in Indian treaty funds entrusted to Indian agent William Logan and an iron strongbox filled with $200,000 in currency as a U.S. Army payroll, accompanied by Major E.W. Eddy. The Brother Jonathan was rumored to have had carried $850,000 in gold (1890 value), $140,000 sent by Wells Fargo & Company and possibly Haskins and Company and $1 million being carried by a New York businessman. Much personal money and jewelry, as well as some of the funds mentioned here, were locked in a large

Dobier safe. Most of the passengers carried currency and gold coins. The *Brother Jonathan*'s treasure probably exceeds $40 million in today's values.

The *Brother Jonathan* left San Francisco for Fort Vancouver, Washington Territory, in spite of Captain Samuel J. De Wolf complaining that it was overloaded. The California Steam Navigation Company's agent told the captain that if he didn't take the *Brother Jonathan* out, the company would find a captain who would. The *Brother Jonathan* stopped at Crescent City briefly to drop cargo off.

The ship left Crescent City Harbor but was unable to make headway in a raging storm. It turned around four miles north of the latitude of Point St. George, about three miles above Crescent City on July 30, 1865, heading for Crescent City Harbor. The *Brother Jonathan* hit Northwest Seal Rock, a rock ledge just one yard above the water surface at low tide, which is part of St. George's Reef.

Of those on board, 213 died, including U.S. Army Brigadier General George Wright, who was going to his new command in the Department of Columbia. Also drowned was a colonel of the Ninth U.S. Infantry Regiment. Only 11 men, 5 women and 3 children in one lifeboat survived. Two other lifeboats were launched but capsized.

Some 170 bodies were recovered, mostly from Pelican Bay, which is north of Crescent City. Sixteen bodies were recovered between Gold Bluffs and Trinidad. Several bodies were found at the entrances to the Rogue River and Smith River. Army paymaster Major Ellery W. Eddy had a premonition that he would die during the trip, and his body was among those recovered.

St. Georges Reef Light Station in 1881. The *Brother Jonathan* sank after hitting this reef in 1865. *Library of Congress.*

Forty-six of the recovered bodies rest at the Crescent City Cemetery. The wreck's wheel and forty feet of the upper deck came ashore near Gold Bluff.

The tug *Mary Ann* from San Francisco quickly arrived but couldn't locate the wreck or retrieve anything. In 1867, 1869, 1872 and the 1890s, salvage groups failed to locate the wreck. In the 1930s, a fisherman caught a Francis Patent lifeboat that probably came from the *Brother Jonathan* in his net. Under the lifeboat seat was a rotting valise with eleven gold bars weighing twenty-two pounds, which would be worth about $500,000 today. Since the U.S. government outlawed gold ownership at that time, the gold bars were hidden and not sold until 1974.

Deep Sea Research Inc. (DSR) discovered the *Brother Jonathan* wreck in October 1993 using its sophisticated equipment. The ship was broken in half at about 275 feet depth off St. George Reef, just southeast of Jonathan Rock near the Dragon Channel. It was about two miles from where it struck the reef. The lower wreck remained intact. DSR filed in court for rights to the wreck's contents under salvage law. A box with 1,207 coins uncirculated, mostly $20 gold pieces, was located and salvaged by DSR. DSR also salvaged numerous bottles, glassware, ceramics, farming equipment and other cargo. The Del Norte County Historical Society has exhibited recovered artifacts. The California's State Lands Commission sued DSR over ownership of the *Brother Jonathan* treasure and artifacts. Although it went to the U.S. Supreme Court, there was a negotiated settlement. DSR received 80 percent of the material, with the remaining 20 percent going to the State of California. About 1,006 gold coins removed from the wreck were sold in auction in 1999 for $5.3 million.

The State of California claimed the wreck of the *Brother Jonathan*, and DSR signed its rights to California as part of its settlement. The large safe and other treasure were never recovered. More than $35 million in current value of gold and other valuables likely are still left on the wreck or in its debris field. While employed by the U.S. Army Corps of Engineers, the author coordinated with federal admiralty attorneys in San Francisco who were determining the federal government's interest in the treasure aboard the *Brother Jonathan.*

Lost Cabin Mine

A prospector was said to have discovered a rich gold vein in the summer of 1859 near where the Klamath River empties into the ocean. He built a cabin and mined the rich ore. Indians attacked him and burned down his cabin. The severely injured prospector made it to a nearby mining camp, where they cared for him. Still injured, he headed back east, but he never returned to California. He told his family and friends about the mine. A group of prospectors traveled to California to look for his burned-down cabin marking the mine site, but they never found it. They reportedly founded the town of Crescent City.

El Dorado County

Chinese Miners' Gold
In the 1870s, near Volcanoville, a mob of drunken miners reportedly drove a group of Chinese miners into a cabin. They murdered the seven to fifteen Chinese miners and set fire to the cabin. Many thought that the murdered Chinese miners had gold hidden near or in the burned-down cabin. In the 1890s, another group of about twelve Chinese mining on the Middle Fork of the American River were killed in a cave-in. The dead miners probably also had gold caches, which have not been found.

Cooper's Lost Cache
In 1864, Diamond Springs miner Edmund Cooper left his placer mine for other gold rushes. He supposedly buried much of his gold at the bottom of an oak tree. Cooper returned to Diamond Springs two years later to find the oak tree cut down. He couldn't even find the tree stump, as a new railroad grade and tracks covered the site. Cooper probed the ground but never found his gold, even though he lived to be over one hundred.

Ebbetts Pass Holdup Loot
See Alpine County.

Forty-Niner's Gold
A forty-niner prospector reportedly found a rich ledge of gold north of Georgetown (previously Growlersburg) and died before showing anyone its location.

Garden Valley Coins
Garden Valley is between Coloma and Georgetown. According to the May 1932 issue of the *Pony Express Courier*, more than $10,000 in gold coins was reportedly buried near the Garden Valley School during the gold rush.

HIRAM NEAL'S GOLD

Prospector Hiram Neal had about five hundred acres near Battle Hill in the 1870s that reportedly had a rich gold vein. He was seventy-five when he showed his family a gallon jar full of gold nuggets. Shortly afterward, he had a stroke. When asked about the jar of nuggets, he said it was nearby. After he died, his family searched the land for years without reporting finding the jar of gold nuggets.

JIM SAVAGE'S CACHE

Major James Savage reportedly had 1,200 Indians working placer gold deposits at Big Oak Flat, where he traded cloth, beads and other goods for the gold. Savage had three trading posts and supposedly had hidden three flour barrels (or one barrel) full of gold nuggets and gold dust. His trading posts were on Mariposa Creek, on the Fresno River and where the Merced River and South Fork of the Merced River join. During a fight in 1852 with his former friend Judge Walter Harvey, he was shot and killed at Poole's Ferry (now Reedley) on the Kings River. Another version of this tale said that Savage died during a robbery. Treasure hunter Michael Paul Henson believed the cache could have been along Fresno Creek west of Coarsegold. This could be in Madera County or Merced County.

JOHN CHAPMAN'S CACHE

John Chapman proudly told people about the $4,000 to $40,000 he reportedly hid near his shack on the edge of the mining camp of Alabama Flat. An unknown person murdered John Chapman one morning during his breakfast at the Alabama Flat House. After John Chapman's funeral, the entire population of Alabama Flats searched unsuccessfully for John Chapman's cache.

LOTUS'S LOST GOLD

An $80,000 gold coin cache was reportedly near Lotus.

PRUITT'S CACHE

In 1910, former slave Tad Trippet worked for rancher Harne Pruitt near Placerville (formerly Hangtown) and reportedly found a half-gallon fruit jar containing fifty-dollar gold slugs while digging a post hole on Pruitt's land. Pruitt took the treasure from him and supposedly cached it twenty-five steps (fifty yards) from Harne Pruitt's barn, which was a few miles from Pilot Hill. Two outlaws tortured Pruitt to get him to disclose its hiding place. He refused, so the robbers killed him. The robbers tortured Trippet, who claimed that he saw Pruitt bury the gold near his barn. The robbers stabbed Trippet and left him for dead without finding the gold.

SALMON FALLS CACHE
Near Salmon Falls on the South Fork of the American River, a crock whiskey jug full of gold coins from a Chinese tong was supposedly cached. Salmon Falls was later covered by Folsom Lake.

TONG TREASURE
Between Blue Canyon and Placerville, within twenty miles of Cedar Springs, $90,000 in gold coins were said to have been hidden among some rocks.

UNIONTOWN GOLD
A successful placer miner supposedly recovered quite a bit of gold near Uniontown (now Lotus). He traded his gold dust and nuggets for gold coins worth $80,000. He didn't trust Wells Fargo or others to transport his gold coins to San Francisco to deposit in a bank. The miner became ill and died. No one knew where he hid his gold.

VOLCANOVILLE TREASURE
Before returning to China to visit, a Chinese merchant sold his store in Volcanoville and buried part of his money and gold somewhere. When he returned back to Volcanoville to recover his money and gold, he could not find the markers, as the town of Volcanoville had burned down in his absence. Over many years, he returned and searched for his treasure, but he never found it.

Old photo of a stagecoach, like the many that carried gold and passengers throughout California. *New York Public Library.*

Wells Fargo Gold
Outlaws robbed a Wells Fargo stagecoach of reportedly $25,000 in gold and cached their loot upstream of Placerville between the South Fork of the American River and the South Fork of the Cosumnes River.

Fresno County

Byrd's Ranch Cache
The Byrd Ranch was between Centerville and Fresno. Byrd told a friend that he hid $60,000 on his ranch near a tree with an old oil can in the fork of two branches. After Byrd died, the story was that the tree was cut down by someone who did not know it was a treasure marker. Years later, while plowing, a farmer found an oil can, and another search for the treasure was made. No one ever reported finding any treasure.

Joaquin Murietta's Tres Piedras and Arroyo Cantoova Treasures
The Tres Piedras (Three Rocks) are buttes about sixteen miles north of Coalinga, where bandit Joaquin Murietta had a hideout. Many have searched for his treasure, which was thought to be nearby. Joaquin Murietta also had a treasure reportedly located in Arroyo Cantoova near Coalinga.

Miner's Lost Mine
A gold miner was murdered for his gold cache, but his gold mine's location was unknown. Some thought that his gold mine was near the South Fork of the Kings River near the Middle Fork of the Kings River junction.

Vásquez Fresno Slough Treasure
One of bandit Tiburcio Vásquez's hideouts was in the community of Los Juntas, where Fresno Slough empties into the San Joaquin River. A legend indicated that Vásquez hid some of his ill-gotten gains near Fresno Slough.

Humboldt County

Eureka Stagecoach Loot
Near Eureka, $123,000 from a stagecoach holdup was supposedly cached.

RATTLESNAKE DICK GANG'S TRINITY MOUNTAIN LOOT
See Trinity County.

SAN FRANCISCO MINT GOLD
A San Francisco Mint employee reportedly stole 290 pounds of gold from the mint and cached it near Shelter Cove—this would be worth more than $7 million today. This is probably a variation of the next story.

SHELTER COVE GOLD
A ship transporting gold to the San Francisco Mint supposedly wrecked in a storm off Shelter Cove. A group of renegade whites and Indians looted the wreck and hid the gold near a tree with the ship's bell in its fork. Soldiers supposedly attacked and killed all the renegades, except for a few women and children. Deer hunters later found the ship's bell and removed it from the tree since they had not heard of the legend. When they hunted for the gold, they didn't find it.

SPANISH MATTOLE RIVER WRECK
An old Spanish ship supposedly sank off the mouth of the Mattole River.

STAGECOACH MYRTLE LOOT
Near Myrtle, robbers may have cached $123,000 in gold from a stagecoach robbery.

WILLOW CREEK LOOT
Robbers stole $23,000 in gold from the Willow Creek Post Office in July 1928 and may have hidden it near Eureka.

WILLOW CREEK LOST MINE
Supposed to be north of Eureka.

IMPERIAL COUNTY

CARRIZO STATION LOOT
One of Juan Murietta's outlaws reportedly stashed loot east of the old Carrizo Stage Station near Carrizo Wash in a cave. This may be a variation of the Church Treasure story that follows.

CHURCH TREASURE

In 1812, a band of Spanish soldiers supposedly landed at Santa Barbara. From there, they marched south into present Mexico and looted several Mexican villages and churches. Their loot reportedly included gold statues, gold, silver, jewelry, altar cloth and a tall solid gold cross that took about twenty men to move.

The Spaniards seized many young Indian girls and were followed by Indians wanting revenge. The Spanish force returned to Alta California. They camped near Sebastian Springs (Harper's Well), where Indians attacked them. The Spaniards reportedly buried ten cartloads of treasure before all but three of the Spaniards died. The rumored cache was said to be within two miles of present California Highway 78 and San Felipe Creek, about one-fourth of a mile upstream of its junction with Carrizo Wash. Two surviving Spaniards were later killed at Barrel Springs. The lone survivor was said to have died between Palm Springs and Indian Wells.

In 1935, an eighty-year-old Indian told the Indian side of the massacre and treasure to a rancher named Henderson. The Indian's father reportedly was with the Indian band that attacked and killed the Spaniards. Henderson passed the story to his friend George Mellor of Hickman, California. For the next twenty years or so, Mellor searched for the treasure. Mellor passed the story down to Vernon D. McCrory of Yuma, Arizona, who died in 1969. Treasure searchers reportedly found human remains and buried carts in the region but have not reported finding any treasure.

FRANCISCO DE ULLOA TREASURE

In 1539, Francisco de Ulloa led a Spanish expedition of discovery along the California coast. De Ulloa supposedly buried Spanish treasure in the Colorado River Delta (in Mexico or Yuma County, Arizona). De Ulloa's treasure in San Diego County was supposedly found. See the TRINIDAD TREASURE, San Diego County, for another De Ulloa treasure.

HANK BRANDT'S LOST MINE

Reportedly in the Superstition Mountains about eighteen miles northwest of El Centro, Hank Brandt mined $4,000 worth of gold each year. When he died before 1941, Brandt reportedly left behind $16,000 in gold. Philip A. Bailey's book *Golden Mirages* described the route to the mine. It is also said to be about fifteen miles from the Carrizo Stage Station—maybe in the Fish Creek Mountains in a canyon. A twin-mouth cave was also mentioned in the story.

LOST BLACK BUTTE MINE
From the Cargo Muchacho Mountains on Black Butte east of Ogilby in 1917, a dehydrated man reached the Southern Pacific Railroad office at Ogilby with seventeen pounds of gold nuggets. He found them in the Algodone Dunes near Grays Well, north of present I-8. During a sandstorm, his mule ran off with his food and water while he was heading for the Cargo Muchacho Mountains. Between two tall sand dunes, he took shelter where bedrock had been exposed by the wind. There he picked up many gold nuggets. From Ogilby he went to Los Angeles, sold his gold nuggets and got ill. Before he died, he gave his doctor a crude map of the location of his find. In 1918, the doctor went to the area but didn't find the lost mine.

LOST DUTCHMAN MINE
An ill prospector with four rich gold ore rocks entered Charles Knowles's camp in Carrizo Wash. The German prospector couldn't remember where he found the ore but claimed that it was nearby. Knowles looked for the site for many years but never found it.

LOST SHIP OF THE DESERT
In about 1610, Captain Alvarez de Cordone led a Spanish naval expedition of three vessels carrying African and native Indian pearl divers up Mexico's Pacific coast. Cordone's expedition gathered many pearls from the Sea of Cortez. One ship sank, and another ship returned to Acapulco when the expedition's commander was wounded in an Indian fight. Captains Juan de Iturbe and Pedro de Rosales continued up the Gulf of California and found the Colorado River Delta. From there, the Spanish ship navigated up the Colorado River to a vast inland sea created when the Colorado River flooded parts of Southern California, including the Salton Sea. The Salton Sea was a much bigger lake at one time called Lake Cahuilla. Dams and irrigation canals now keep these lowlands from becoming a lake. The last time the Colorado River overflowed into the area was 1905. The Salton Sea continues to shrink due to water diversions and drought.

The Spaniards believed that they found a channel to the Pacific Ocean, as California was then thought to be a large island. The inland lake got shallower as the ship looked for a passage to the north. The floodwater receded and stranded the ship, which supposedly had a treasure of gold and silver in addition to the pearls.

The legend claimed that De Iturbe and his crew left most of their treasure aboard the vessel. In the fall of 1615, De Iturbe and his men finally reached Spanish settlements. When several Spanish navy expeditions returned to the Colorado River mouth, they were not able to sail up the then shallow Colorado River.

The inland sea mostly dried up. The grounded ship disappeared beneath shifting sand. The Kane Springs area as well as San Felipe Creek, southwest of the southern portion of the Salton Sea, are regions where it was said the sands moved and exposed the remains of the ship.

In 1775, a Spanish muleskinner and prospector, Jesus Espinoza, scouted the Chocolate Mountains looking for passes and trails that Juan Bautista de Anza's expedition could use for a new road between present Yuma, Arizona, and Los Angeles. In a gorge through the towering cliffs, Espinoza reportedly found a rock carved like an Indian's head. He entered the ravine, dismounted and traveled by foot to a natural archway about twenty feet in diameter. Espinoza used footholds to climb a rock wall and reach the arch. Through the arch, he saw a large salt desert with an odd, dark shape in the distance. He descended to the desert floor on the west side of the mountains. He claimed that he reached the ship, which still had masts, but the bow was partially buried in the salt plain. He entered the rotting hold and found large numbers of pearls. Espinoza supposedly gathered what treasure he could carry and traveled toward the arch. He noticed unusual rock formations, including one with a giant face directly in front of the ship. He reached his horse and headed for the Spanish settlements along the California coast.

Jesus Espinoza found a gap in the ridge he could ride through far south of where he had originally crossed the ridge line on foot at the arch. Espinoza rode to Mission San Diego de Alcalá, where he told his tale of the lost ship. He used the pearls for money. He and two Indians and two Spaniards later searched for the lost ship.

In 1870, prospector Charley Clusker got people to bankroll him to search for the wreck after he reported a sighting about forty-five to fifty miles southwest of Dos Palmas, just south of the Salton Sea. The *San Bernardino Guardian* reported that the ship in the desert was two hundred feet long and filled with gold coins and pearls—an obvious lie. The conclusion was that Charley Clusker was prospecting with other people's money. Some thought that maybe he found the ship, but it had no treasure.

One man reportedly recovered a chest from the ship's decaying timbers. A 1907 story claimed that the wreck was about six miles east of Imperial.

LOST PICACHO PEAK SPANISH MINE/MISSION TREASURE

Near Picacho Peak (Sugarloaf Mountain), a Spanish mine was reportedly worked by Indians from the two Spanish pueblos and missions on the Colorado River near present Yuma, Arizona. In the fall of 1780, opposite Yuma, Mission La Purisima Concepcion was founded. About four leagues downstream on the Colorado River, Mission San Pedro y San Pablo de Bicuñer was also built. Both missions were founded by Padre Francisco Garcês, and three other padres, along with about fifty colonists, workers, soldiers and their families. The Spanish mined placer gold deposits in the Imperial Valley from around 1775 to 1780 in the Potholes District, Picacho District and Cargo Muchacho-Tumco District. According to Native American Indian traditions, the Indians were treated like slaves and forced to mine gold.

On July 17, 1781, the Yuma Indians (Quechans) revolted against the Spanish. The Indians attacked the two Spanish missions, killing Franciscan Padre Francisco Garcês, three other padres and most of the Spaniards. The captured Spanish men, women and children were eventually rescued and traveled to the safety of Sonora.

Two Americans, Thomas Russell and Peter Weldon, and Mexican Francisco Ruiz left San Diego in 1836 to look for rumored lost Spanish treasure said to be near Yuma. When the trio returned to San Diego, the Mexican authorities arrested, jailed and tried them for looking for treasure without a license, even though they don't appear to have actually found any treasure.

Over the centuries, treasure hunters dug up the old missions' foundations looking for gold caches. Fort Yuma was later built on the site of Mission La Purisma Concepcion. The other mission was reportedly uncovered and bisected by the All American Canal just downstream of the Laguna Dam. A legend claimed that the Yuma Indians buried gold from a lost Spanish mine on the Arizona side of the Colorado River. Other legends claimed that the Indians threw mined gold into the Colorado River or that they buried it near the base of Picacho Peak.

SPANISH PLACER GOLD TREASURE

Gold from Spanish placer mines worked by the Yuma (Quechan) Indians was being transported when the party was said to have been ambushed by Indians. The attack was at a narrow point in the trail near the Indian shrine of E-Vee-Taw-Ash, about nineteen miles north of Yuma in the Chocolate Mountains. All the Spaniards were killed. The Indians supposedly dumped the captured gold into a cave.

Scene from a stagecoach robbery, with both the stagecoach cargo and passengers being robbed. *National Park Service.*

STAGECOACH CARRIZO LOOT

In the 1860s, a special stagecoach carried a gold shipment ($350,000) from El Paso, Texas, bound for San Diego. At Yuma, the stagecoach guard suddenly got sick and stayed behind. Near the Imperial County/San Diego County line, east of the Carrizo Stage Station, a lone robber held up the stagecoach and wounded the stagecoach driver. The robber took the gold coins. As the robber was riding off, the driver shot and wounded him. Near the holdup site, the outlaw's body was later found, but the loot was missing. There could have been an accomplice who took the gold, or perhaps the gold was buried by the outlaw before he died. This treasure could be in San Diego County.

TRAVERTINE ROCK TREASURE

In about 1750, a French and Spanish bandit band supposedly moved their loot from Mexican churches as Indians followed them. The bandits hid their loot in a cave near Travertine Rock, south of the Riverside County/Imperial County line. The Indians attacked and killed all the bandits. Travertine Rock contains an inscription of an old papal cross and a cross of Lorraine, which may be how this legend got started.

INYO COUNTY

ALKALI JONES'S LOST GOLD

Prospector Alkali Jones reportedly found gold-bearing milky white quartz at a butte between Skidoo and Searchlight when he was in a sandstorm. Some think that it was in the Black Hills, Ryan and Greenwooton Range Area. It could be between Jubilee Pass and Funeral Peak. He called his mine Golden Eagle. Jones carried nine pounds of gold ore, which he sold for $180 to buy supplies and burros. He left to return to his mine and vanished.

BANDIT DEATH VALLEY CACHE

In Death Valley, about eight miles north of Jayhawker Spring, bandits reportedly attacked a party carrying $16,000 in gold coins. The loot was cached in a narrow canyon.

Prospector with his burro hunting for a gold bonanza. *Library of Congress.*

Death Valley Ranch is a garden spot in the harsh Death Valley. Many tales of lost mines abound in Death Valley. *Library of Congress.*

CHARLIE'S BUTTE TREASURE

Paiute Indians attacked two wagons near Fish Springs in the Owens Valley. A man named Charlie held off the Indians while the rest of the small party escaped. Charlie was killed, so a nearby peak was named after him. About $1,000 in gold coins was reportedly on the wagons. Some believe that the gold was left behind when the wagons were burned.

"DEATH VALLEY" SCOTTY TREASURES

"Death Valley" Scotty (Walter Edward Perry Scott) supposedly hid $7,000 in gold dust in or near his castle. There is also a story that he hid twenty-five $1,000 bills in Scotty's Castle. Despite the name, Scotty did not own the structure. Millionaire Albert Mussey Johnson owned what is called Scotty's Castle and the ranch around it. Scotty was a prospector, promoter and con man who promoted nonexistent mines to investors. Scotty's Castle is in Death Valley National Park.

FOUND DEATH VALLEY CHEST

On November 22, 1985, archaeologist Jerry Freeman was following a gold rush trail through Death Valley National Park in the Panament Mountains when he investigated two caves along the route. Inside the deepest cave, Freeman found an old chest that was thirty-one inches by nineteen inches by twelve inches high. Inside the chest was a dated January 2, 1850 manifest of its contents written by forty-niner William Robinson, who had died on the trek before he reached the gold fields. The chest contained $52.75 face value in eighty coins, including $5 and $10 gold pieces and silver dollars. These coins were older than 1850. Also inside the chest were tintypes, ceramics, a pistol, a powder horn and other items. Freeman and others helped him remove the chest, and he later handed it over to staff of the National Park Service, who were appalled that it had been removed. The National Park Service examined the trunk and its contents and claimed that it was a fraud. They said that the letter was a forgery and that there was twentieth-century glue on three items. A modern adhesive from a sticker was found on a bowl.

INDIAN GOLD NECKLACES
Mummies in an Indian burial were said to have had gold nugget necklaces in the Coso Range near China Lake.

INDIAN OCTAGONAL GOLD
Indians reportedly stole octagonal gold coins and hid them in a cleft rock not far from a spring. This was possibly cached in the northern Death Valley area, in the Tucki Mountains or maybe at Anza Borrego.

JAYHAWKER EMIGRANT CACHES
Members of a Jayhawker emigrant wagon train supposedly cached their treasure at an area seven miles southwest of Emigrant Springs, at a Tucki Mountains pass and in the White Sage Flats.

JAYHAWKER SPRING TREASURE
An emigrant party reportedly buried about $2,000 in gold and silver coins near Jayhawker Spring in 1849.

LOST ALEC RAMY'S MINE
Alec Ramy's mine was supposedly in the Last Chance Mountains on the south slope of Dry Mountain.

Desolate and hot Death Valley as seen from Furnace Creek. *New York Public Library*.

Lost Breyfogle Mine

In the story of the famous Lost Breyfogle Mine, Charles Breyfogle was sometimes confused with his brother Jacob Breyfogle and his cousin William O. Breyfogle. In J. Frank Dobie's *Coronado's Children*, three prospectors named Breyfogle, McLeod and O'Bannon left Los Angeles via the Mohave Desert in early 1862 for a new silver strike near Austin, Nevada Territory. Another legend has Breyfogle being with a group of Confederate sympathizers in 1863 or 1864 going through and then returning to Los Angeles.

From Los Angeles, Breyfogle left with McLeod and O'Bannon for Austin. Harry Sinclair Drago's *Lost Bonanzas* has a version of this tale taking place in 1864 with three pro-Confederates and Breyfogle riding to join the Confederate army by going south from Austin, Nevada Territory, down the Old Spanish Trail to San Bernardino and Yuma, where they would head into Mexico and then travel east to Confederate Texas. Breyfogle supposedly joined the Confederates at Ash Meadows or Mesquite Springs, about thirty miles northwest of Stovepipe Wells.

They traveled through the eastern side of the Panamint Range, near Death Valley, where they camped for the night. Drago wrote that the campsite was between Stovepipe Wells and Daylight Springs on the east side of the Funeral Mountains.

That night, Indians killed McLeod and O'Bannon while Breyfogle slept several hundred yards away from his two companions. A variation of this legend claimed that Breyfogle was partially scalped. A barefoot Breyfogle raced downslope into Death Valley. As he climbed up the Funeral Range, he later remembered seeing green to the south, about three miles away.

Breyfogle walked toward the green area, thinking that it was a spring, as he was dying of thirst. About halfway to the green vegetation, he stumbled across some gray float with gold. Breyfogle then found reddish feldspar rich in gold. Breyfogle picked up a few ore samples and put them in his bandanna. Somehow he reached the green vegetation, which was a mesquite tree. He quickly ate mesquite beans and collapsed. One story claimed that Breyfogle was attacked and clubbed unconscious by Indians while sleeping at a spring. The Indians reportedly stole most of Breyfogle's clothes and left him to die. Breyfogle managed to reach a spring known as Coyote Holes.

Most stories agreed that Breyfogle walked through Death Valley to near Austin, Nevada Territory. At Baxter Springs, Nevada Territory, some 260 miles north of where he last remembered being, Breyfogle finally returned to normal and recovered his memory. Another version claimed that he was found on the Old Spanish Trail by travelers, more than one hundred miles from Death Valley. Another variation had rancher Wilson finding Breyfogle in Big Smokey Valley, Nevada Territory, after Breyfogle crossed the Funeral Range and Amargosa Desert.

When Breyfogle reached Austin, he was still carrying rich pink feldspar gold ore samples, which caused a sensation. That winter, Breyfogle and twenty men searched for his lost mine. Breyfogle found the mesquite tree that saved his life but not his lost ledge. For many years, Breyfogle led prospecting parties looking for his lost gold ledge in the Hiko area. Until Breyfogle died in 1870, he worked in the Austin and Eureka, Nevada mining districts. Other stories claim that Paiute Indians traded similar-looking gold at Nevada trading posts for goods they needed. Over the centuries, hundreds have searched for the Lost Breyfogle Mine, with some searchers dying in the torrid Funeral Range.

Two prospectors named Higgins and Covington supposedly were led by a friendly Indian in 1880 to a cave containing a large amount of gold, which could have been from the Lost Breyfogle Mine. Hostile Indians prevented the two prospectors from returning to the site. They gave up the search in about 1900. This mine could have been located in Nye County, Nevada. The area where the Lost Breyfogle Mine was believed located has had a number of rich mines over the years. One of these rich mines could have been Breyfogle's.

Lost Galler-Tauber Diggings

Germans John Galler and Wolfgang Tauber were partners who found a rich placer deposit in early 1850 at a spring on a gulch that ran into Wingate Wash in the Panamint Mountain Range. Both were starving and without water when they found the spring. They picked up gold nuggets, left the gulch and found their way to Camulos Rancho of Ignacio de Valle, where they recovered before continuing to Los Angeles. In Los Angeles, they prospered as merchants. Tauber got on a ship and died before he could return to Germany. In the 1860s, Galler reportedly left Los Angeles to hunt for his lost mine, but he gave up the search. Many gold discoveries were made by others in the area, so his lost diggings may have been found.

Lost Goler Diggings

A German hunter and prospector called John Goler supposedly found a rich mine near a spring and stuck his Spencer rifle in a small hill to serve as a marker. He became lost and disoriented. The site was reportedly at Goler Wash on the west slope of the Panamint Mountain Range. It's said to be in Goler Canyon (Galler Canyon) about thirty-two miles north of Mohave, near Cantil. It may be in the lower El Paso Mountains close to Randsburg. Goler led several expeditions to look for the gold but never found it. The Spencer rifle was reportedly found in 1917 on top of a hill by owners of the Lazy M Ranch close to Red Rock Canyon. This area produced a lot of placer gold, so it's likely that this lost mine was found and depleted. Delos Toole's article discussed confusion between the Lost Galler Diggings (John Galler) and Lost Goler Diggings (John Goler), as perhaps they were different mines found by different people in the same area.

Lost Gunsight Mine

A Kansas Jayhawker who was part of the Georgia-Mississippi Party in 1849 discovered a rich silver ledge and used some of the silver to make a rifle gunsight. Several locations mentioned include the northwest part of Emigrant Wash, White Sage Flats, near a mesa between Emigrant Canyon, Wild Rose Canyon, between Emigrant Pass and Searles Dry Lake and in Nemo Canyon on the Death Valley side of the Tucki Mountains. Other locations are the Panamint Mountains in the lower part of Butte Valley or on the east side of the Amagosa Mountains not far from White Sage Flats. This could be in Nevada. This could also be San Bernardino County.

Lost Jack Steward Mine

Supposedly between Stovepipe Wells and Olancha, possibly near Calico Mountain, prospector Jack Stewart found gold-laced quartz at the bottom of a wash. He did not return to it but told a friend about it before dying in 1947.

Lost Oriflamme Mountain Nuggets

An Indian cowboy and his young cowboy friend were driving cattle with the boss when one night the Indian picked up some gold nuggets near Oriflamme Mountain while at camp. The Indian told the young cowboy there were other deposits nearby. The young cowboy was unable to relocate the area when his Indian friend lost touch with him. These deposits may still be there to find.

Lost Paiute Cave

Several boys were said to have found a tunnel-like cave in the side of a mountain. Water flowed through the cave, which contained rich gold deposits in sand. This is possibly between Stovepipe Wells and Grapevine Ridge.

MADAM'S GOLD

A madam who ran a house of ill repute reportedly stashed her gold coins in five-gallon kerosene cans. She was murdered by robbers trying to get her gold. "Death Valley" Scotty and Walter Blake reportedly hunted for this gold in Death Valley.

OWENS LAKE TREASURE

The steamer *Mollie Stevens* supposedly sank in Owens Lake with $200,000 in gold and silver ore or silver bars (from the Cerro-Gordo Mine) in 1897, with its crew of four all killed. Since then, Owens Lake has now mostly dried up and is farmed. Other stories include a wagon load of ore that rolled off a ship during a storm. Moving ore across Owens Lake was a shortcut to get the silver to market.

SCOTTY'S LOST GOLD MINE

Reportedly, "Death Valley" Scotty's gold mine was near Scotty's Castle in northern Death Valley. Scotty promoted nonexistent mines, so this lost mine is probably false. Several of Scotty's lost mines were said to be in this area. A judge ruled in 1941 that Scotty's gold mine was a fabrication. Scotty died in January 1954.

KERN COUNTY

CACHE CREEK TREASURE

Indians attacked a wagon train on the downward side of Tehachapi Pass when some of the wagon train members fled up Cache Creek and reportedly cached $15,000 in gold coins before being killed. Survivors of the attack knew that the others had gold but did not know where they had hidden it.

GEORGE ELY CACHE

George Ely stayed at Glenville and was rumored to have hidden his wealth there.

GREENHORN GULCH CACHE

The owner of a store and saloon at the Greenhorn Gulch (Creek) and Freeman Gulch (Creek) junction between Democrat Hot Springs and Miracle Hot Springs near the Kern River supposedly cached his money nearby.

He told family that he had hidden more than $100,000 in caches near his establishment. After he died in a mine cave-in, his family found about $48,000 in coins and gold dust in glass jars. The rest may be hidden still.

HORSE CANYON CACHE

Near a Horse Canyon spring, Indians reportedly hid loot from a wagon train raid in a cave or nearby.

INDIAN GREENHORN MOUNTAIN CACHE

When illness struck a party of Indians and killed most of them, they reportedly cached gold, silver, weapons and their valuables north of the Kern River on Greenhorn Mountain in Freeman Gulch near the Davis Ranger Station.

LAKE ISABELLA MINER CACHE

Near his hut overlooking and just north of Isabella, a miner supposedly hid his fortune of a few thousand dollars. He died of blood poisoning, and his cache has never been found. This site may be near Lake Isabella.

LOST MISSION MINE/LOS PADRES MINE/LOST PADRE PLACER

See Ventura County.

MASON-HENRY GANG LOOT

During the American Civil War in the San Joaquin Valley, a gang of pro-Confederate outlaws ranged. The gang reportedly had a Tejon Canyon hideout. The steep, treacherous trail to their hideout was as narrow as three feet wide between rocks. Legend has it that at the end of the trail, the outlaw gang leader Mason buried a saddlebag and money belt from a Techachapi robbery.

PROSPECTOR'S GOLD

In the Greenhorn Mountains, a prospector reportedly buried a six-foot-long drainpipe containing gold nuggets near Glennville.

ROBBERS ROOST CACHES

A treasure hunter reportedly uncovered a cache of about $12,000 in gold coins in 1957 in an area near an outlaw gang's 1873 robbery near Ridgecrest. Soldiers following behind the stagecoach reportedly killed all the outlaws. Before the last outlaw was killed, he hid the gold. Mexican outlaws supposedly hid $40,000 in gold near Vasquez Rocks, about a mile from Freeman Raymond's stage station (Freeman Wash) or Walker Pass. The Vasquez Rocks are located in the Sierra Pelona Mountains on an Escondido Canyon ridge, about four miles northwest of Acton. A strongbox with $25,000 (or $50,000) in gold was said to have been washed away with a stagecoach during a storm a few miles north of Robber's Roost a half mile from Freeman Junction. Freeman Raymond's stage station was nearby. Freeman Raymond operated the stage station and supposedly buried his $80,000 in gold fortune south of his stage station in a wash. These tales could be variations of the same treasure story for the most part. See the REPETTO TREASURE in Los Angeles County. The Vasquez Rocks have appeared as the backdrop for many movies and television shows, as they are quite dramatic.

MISSION SAN BUENAVENTURA TREASURE
Some Indians were said to have carried Spanish church treasure from Mission San Buenaventura over the mountains to hide it near Lake Buena Vista. Mission San Buenaventura was established in 1782. In 1824, mission Indians fled Mission San Buenaventura and were pursued by soldiers to near Lake Buena Vista, so maybe they took church treasure with them.

SPANISH CARRETA TREASURE
Indians supposedly attacked and killed a small group of men with a *carreta* (cart) of treasure in a small canyon near present Boron. Gold coins from the *carreta* reportedly were buried. The *carreta* was rolled over the cache and set afire to hide the cache. This could be located in San Bernardino County.

KING COUNTY

LOST VISALIA MEXICAN MINE
This lost mine was reportedly about sixty miles north of Visalia.

LAKE COUNTY

PAYROLL CACHE
See Napa County.

Lassen County

Bloody Springs Treasure
At Bloody Springs, Indians massacred an emigrant train a few miles southeast of Pittsville on the Pit River. The lone surviving emigrant made it to Fort Crook to tell his tale. The Indians supposedly found much gold aboard the wagons and threw $20 gold pieces into the Pit River or across Pit Gorge. Some $20 gold pieces have been reportedly found in the area. Another version of this tale claimed that $60,000 in treasure was hidden.

Brockman's Lost Mine
While rounding up his horses southwest of Horse Lake, Brockman halted at a small creek to let his horse drink. He saw black quartz on the creek bank and picked up a piece. It turned out to be rich in gold. A storm hit, and he detoured to Susanville before it snowed. Later, he searched for the site but couldn't find it.

Honey Lake Treasure
See Plumas County.

Joaquin Murietta Fredonyer Pass Cache
Bandit Joaquin Murietta supposedly cached $200,000 in loot between Fredonyer Pass and Susanville.

Captain Dick's Gold Nuggets
See Modoc County.

Outlaw Skinner's Cache
Outlaw George Skinner supposedly cached $35,000 in gold bars in 1856 near Horse Lake on the west side of Trinity Mountain.

Los Angeles County

Ada Hancock's Treasure
The eighty-three-ton twin screw steam tug *Ada Hancock* was sixty-six feet long and built in 1858 in San Francisco. On April 27, 1863, it was ferrying sixty passengers and at least $45,000 from the San Pedro wharf (Banning Dock) to

the waiting San Francisco–bound steamer *Senator*. The *Senator* was anchored near Dead Man's Island (now dredged away) in Wilmington Harbor. The *Ada Hancock* suddenly exploded about one thousand yards from shore when water rushed into the boiler room as the ship rolled and allowed water to enter it.

Some thought that it was no accident, as gunshots were heard by some survivors before the explosion (the ship had gunpowder aboard). It sank with twenty-six dead and thirty-seven injured, of which twenty-three later died.

Two fatalities were Wells Fargo messenger William Ritchie, with $10,000 to $125,000 in gold, and Fred E. Kerlin of Fort Tejon, who had $30,000 in greenbacks. Nothing was listed as being recovered. The area has had a lot of dredging and jetties built over the years, as in 1863 deep-draft ships had to anchor far off the port.

ARROYO SECO TREASURE

A family's treasure was placed in two boxes by the father and reportedly buried near Arroyo Seco Canyon's mouth. The father may have reburied it later, as his son couldn't find the boxes. A rock with a cross carved on it was a marker for the burial site.

CAHUENGA PASS LOOT

Loot from the robbery of a Hollywood bank was said to be hidden in the Cahuenga Pass area.

Warships like this traveled along the California coast during the Spanish colonial days. The offshore Channel Islands and reefs caused some to wreck. *National Archives.*

Dead Man's Cove Caches

At Dead Man's Cove near Portuguese Bend, west of San Pedro, Mexican jewelry as well as gold and silver coins were reportedly cached in a metal box. Other caches were rumored to be in this area, as smugglers and pirates used Dead Man's Cove and the Palos Verdes area.

Dodger Stadium Treasure

Another rumored Spanish treasure was buried in Los Angeles's Dodger Stadium area. During the stadium's construction, some rocks with Spanish markings were found. This caused some to suspect that a Spanish treasure was cached nearby.

Dominguez Rancho Treasure

During the Mexican-American War, at the Dominguez Rancho, a Mexican treasure may have been cached. The Dominguez Rancho later became a Claretian Order seminary.

Don Avila's Gold

In 1818, Don Francisco de Avila constructed an adobe home in Los Angeles on what is now Olvera Street. Don Avila's descendants reported that when he sold cattle and sheep, he cached the money in or near his adobe. He was also said to have placed the gold coins in tin cans and buried them under a pepper tree. In 1831, Don Avila died, and the secret of where he hid his money died with him. During the Mexican-American War, U.S. Navy commodore Robert F. Stockton occupied Don Avila's home and used it as the California capitol during the American conquest of California in 1847. It is the oldest house in Los Angeles.

Don Juan's Gold

In 1810, rich Spanish mine owner Don Juan supposedly left Guadalupe, Mexico, with a caravan bound for Alta California. Don Juan's caravan reportedly included sixty horses, many Indian servants and gold. They crossed the Colorado River near the Gila River junction. Between Signal Hill and Carrizo, a large number of Indians attacked the caravan. During the moving battle, Don Juan's gold was said to have been hidden in a small arroyo. Don Juan and everyone in the caravan were killed, and his gold was lost. The area near Signal Hill is mentioned as a possible cache site.

DON TIBURCIO TAPIA TREASURES

Don Tiburcio Tapia was born in 1789 and served as a Spanish soldier and politician. He received a large Spanish land grant for his services to the Crown. Tapia constructed a large hacienda on a hill east of Pamona. Tapia also established the Cucamonga Ranch and winery. In 1804, the Spanish king granted Rancho Malibu (present-day Malibu) to Jose Barolome Tapia, one of Don Tapia's relatives. Tiburcio Tapia had a store in Los Angeles and reportedly made a fortune smuggling goods ashore at Santa Catalina Island when California was off-limits to foreign imports. Californio Don Tiburcio Tapia supported Mexico's independence from Spain. He reportedly buried some of his treasure when Governor Manuel Micheltorena came to California to put down a possible Californio revolt.

In 1846, U.S. Army forces under John C. Frémont reached Southern California. Don Tapia reportedly hid his life savings to avoid robbery or confiscation. Don Tapia had collected treasure to build a chapel at Cucamonga. Don Tapia and his son Ramon reportedly buried two steel caskets weighing 117 pounds each with 3,125 Spanish coins at Arroyo Seco. Large rocks were arranged to form a cross near Rancho San Jose de Ariba, at Pomona or Red Hill, on the east side of the valley under a huge tree. Another legend had Don Tapia burying part of his treasure near Malibu Village in Rancho Malibu. There is also a tale that he buried a brass-bound chest containing gold and silver coins on his Cucamonga Ranch. One of Don Tapia's treasures could also be located in San Bernardino County.

On his deathbed in 1848, Don Tapia reportedly gave incomplete instructions to his sons on where he hid his fortune. His treasures reportedly were never found by his family.

In December 1877, two young Mexican workers digging along Arroyo Seco near Monterey Park found an old chest containing $300 in old Mexican pesos along with several bags of gold dust, gold doubloons and jewelry (worth between $30,000 and $50,000 then). Many believe that this treasure was part of Don Tapia's fortune. Also in Malibu, a kettle half full of gold and silver coins was found during building construction. This cache may have belonged to Don Tapia.

DUARTE'S LOST GOLD

Near Pamona, Andres Duarte was said to have cached gold coins on his four-thousand-acre ranch, which included his adobe. When American forces took over California in the Bear Flag Revolt and Mexican-American War, Duarte fled south to Mexico. He eventually returned, and the last of his sons lived in the area until 1893, supposedly looking for his father's caches. There was much digging for many years by people hunting the cache.

DUNCAN RANCH CACHE
Near Manhattan Beach is the Duncan Ranch Cache.

ELYSIAN PARK TREASURE
There are several versions about whether a wealthy Spanish family or a pirate cached a rumored $6 million treasure in the Elysian Park region of Los Angeles.

FISH CANYON MINE
Where Fish Canyon joins San Gabriel Wash, about twelve miles northeast of Mission San Gabriel de Archangel, there may have been a padre placer mine. Mission San Gabriel de Archangel padres reportedly had Indians mine placer gold in this area.

FOREST LAWN TREASURES
During a January 1963 trial, there was testimony by Fran Campbell from Burbank that Spanish conquistadors buried millions in treasure in hills in the Forest Lawn Memorial Park area. She also said that Carlos Vasques robbed the San Fernando Bank around 1890 in the same area and hid his loot.

JOAQUIN MURIETTA SAN FERNANDO VALLEY LOOT
The bandit Joaquin Murietta reportedly cached $34,000 in loot in the San Fernando Valley, possibly on the Albert Workman Ranch.

LA CANADA DE MOLINO MINE
Gold mined from La Canada de Molino (Mill Creek) Mine supposedly was transported to Mission San Fernando Rey de España (Saint Ferdinand, King of Spain). This mine was reportedly on Mill Creek near Big Tujunga in the San Gabriel Mountains. In fact, gold has been mined in an area near Big Tujunga northeast of San Fernando. Some speculate that the Monte Cristo Mine from the 1880s was this old Spanish mine.

LIZZARD HEAD ROCK LOOT
In 1875, the Ventura to Encino stagecoach was robbed in the western San Fernando Valley in the Santa Susanna Mountains. The loot was reportedly cached near Lizzard Head Rock.

An old trading post in Columbia, Tuolumne County. *Library of Congress.*

LOST CLAREMONT INDIAN GOLD MINE

In the San Gabriel Mountains near Claremont, there was a legend about a lost Indian mine. Mission San Gabriel de Archangel Indians discovered a deposit of gold north of the mission. An Indian reportedly recovered gold nuggets in the San Gabriel Mountains north of Pasadena and spent them on liquor. From the town, the Indian was trailed to the Pasadena foothills, where he evaded those following him. Outlaws murdered him when he refused to show them where his gold mine was located. Some claimed that this lost Indian mine was near Mount Disappointment. Small gold deposits have been found north of Claremont, but the Indian's gold mine may still be undiscovered.

LOST MEXICAN JUARISTA TREASURE

General Placido Vega y Daza was a Mexican agent for Benito Juárez's government during the Mexican war against France's occupation. Explorer Christopher Columbus was an ancestor of General Vega. Vega was a former Mexican governor. In 1861 (this date is suspect), Vega supposedly transported gold, silver and jewels worth $200,000 ($400,000 in another version) to Southern California to buy weapons for Benito Juárez's army. Three men reportedly robbed Vega of the Mexican treasure and cached it in the San Bruno hills in San Mateo County. Vega was mentioned in the "Official Records" as being an agent who bought guns for the Juarista government during the Civil War.

From a hiding place, sheepherder Diego Moreno supposedly saw the robbers cache the Juarista treasure. Moreno dug up the treasure ($20,000).

In Los Angeles near a tavern at present Cahuenga Boulevard and Highland Avenue, on the southern portion of Cahuenga Pass, Moreno supposedly buried the stolen Juarista treasure in six separate caches around a Fresno tree.

Diego Moreno became ill while in Los Angeles and was taken care of by Jesus Martinez. Moreno told Martinez about the treasure before dying. Jesus Martinez and his son went to Cahuenga Pass and found the Fresno tree, but before they could dig up the treasure, Jesus Martinez fell dead. The young Martinez decided that the treasure was cursed, so he reportedly left the site without digging up the treasure.

In 1885, a dog dug up a small buckskin bag and took it to a Basque sheepherder named Correo. The buckskin bag was part of General Vega's Mexican treasure. Correo became a wealthy man who returned to Spain. In 1939, the County of Los Angeles issued two mining engineers a permit to hunt for the Juarista treasure in a Hollywood Bowl parking lot, but they found nothing.

Documents show that General Vega was a Mexican agent from 1864 to 1866 based out of San Francisco. He arrived in California from Mexico in 1864 with $262,578.79 in cash and letters of credit. While in California, he raised money for the Juarista government by getting loans, making deals on Mexican resource concessions, receiving donations from sympathetic Hispanics and similar activities. He paid about $620,000 for more than twenty thousand rifles, millions of cartridges and other military hardware for the Juarista government. He used money to buy influence for the Juarista government's war against French occupation and its Mexican supporters. Some Juarista funds may have been stolen, as there was much intrigue at the time. Once the French were driven from Mexico and the Juaristas took over, Vega was accused of misuse of funds. Vega never held another Mexican high political office.

McNALLY RANCH LOOT
Near Norwalk, the McNally Ranch loot was supposedly hidden.

MIGUEL LEONIS TREASURE
Basque sheepherder Miguel Leonis (or Leone) was said to have hidden his fortune in an area near Calabasas before he died on September 20, 1889. Numerous lawsuits were made over his estate. Possibly his fortune was hidden in the area of his adobe, which was constructed in 1844. His home was restored as the Leonis Adobe Museum. No one knew where he cached his treasure. It could be in gold coins, according to some stories.

MISSION SAN FERNANDO TREASURES

A Spanish party with a cart carrying gold reportedly traveled from Mission San Fernando Rey de España heading for San Pedro when Indians or a gang of robbers attacked them. At the mouth of Santa Ynez Canyon, where Sunset Boulevard now joins the Pacific Highway (California Highway 1), the Spaniards reportedly dumped the treasure in a marsh or small lake. When Sunset Boulevard was constructed, the lake and wetlands were filled in. In 1842, ranch foreman Francisco Lopez at Mission San Fernando Rey de Espana pulled onions from a garden for his lunch and discovered gold flakes in the garden soil. A gold rush began but ended a few months later after very little additional gold was recovered.

MISSION SAN GABRIEL ARCHANGEL TREASURES

The original site of Mission San Gabriel Archangel was founded in 1771, but Indians attacked it one month after its founding, as Spanish soldiers reportedly raped an Indian woman. In 1775, the mission was moved to its current site. One legend claimed that gold from nearby mines was hidden in the mission courtyard. As late as 1936, it was claimed that mission padres hunted for the gold. A legend also claimed that there was an escape tunnel at the mission hiding the padres' gold treasure. In the early 1930s, a group of treasure hunters led by a spirit searched for a treasure taken from Mission San Gabriel Archangel at Coyote Pass in the Monterey Park area.

MULHOLLAND DRIVE BRIEFCASE

Between Sepulveda Canyon and Coldwater Canyon, a lawyer with $45,000 in his briefcase thought that he was being followed so he reportedly threw it out of his car in 1932. The briefcase with the cash was never found.

NUESTRA SENORA DE AYUDA

The Spanish 230-ton Manila galleon *Nuestra Senora de Ayuda* sank in 1641 with a reported treasure of $500,000 when it ran onto a rock west of Santa Catalina Island and capsized. Some believe that the wreck is in the Outer Santa Barbara Channel.

PASADENA TREASURES

Near Pasadena, a Spanish mission's gold bullion was reportedly buried near present Armada Drive and Zanja Street. During an Indian revolt, a Mexican family treasure totaling 600,000 pesos was supposedly buried near the site of the Huntington-Sheraton Hotel, located on 1401 South Oak Knoll Drive, and never recovered.

REPETTO TREASURE

On April 14, 1874, Tiburcio Vásquez and his gang looted Alessandro Repetto's ranch. Repetto had immigrated to California from Italy and amassed a fortune on his five-thousand-acre ranch at King's Hills in Monterey Park. Vásquez demanded Repetto's fortune and threatened to murder him. Repetto claimed that his money was in a Los Angeles bank. Repetto sent a boy to the bank to get $800. At the bank, the boy told the banker and sheriff about the Vásquez Gang's robbery. As the Los Angeles posse rode to Repetto's ranch, the Vásquez Gang drank Repetto's wine and looted his ranch. After being tortured, Repetto supposedly handed over $40,000 in gold and silver coins to the gang.

The approaching Los Angeles posse was sighted by Vásquez's guards. The Vásquez Gang fled into the hills, where many believe they hid the treasure. The loot supposedly was cached near Monterey Park, San Gabriel, Montebello, near Chatsworth ($130,000 by one tale), in San Francisco Canyon and near the Vásquez Rocks. For many years, Repetto hunted for the burial site of his fortune before selling his estate and dying. By 1927, his ranch home had become a ruin after being destroyed by time and treasure hunters. See ROBBERS ROOST CACHES, Kern County.

SAN CARLOS

In March 1797, the vessel *San Carlos* carrying gold and jewelry reportedly sank during a storm in the Santa Barbara Channel.

SAN PEDRO

The Spanish galleon *San Pedro* reportedly carried $4 million (or $3 million) in gold and silver bullion, along with coins from Panama when a Dutch warship spotted it and gave chase. The *San Pedro* fled northward and was damaged in a storm. Off Arrow Point (Ship Rock), Santa Catalina Island, on July 4, 1598, the Spanish ship hit a reef and sank in eighty-four feet of water. The majority of its crew reached shore and were rescued. Francisco Pedilla tried to salvage the galleon in 1602, but horrible storms killed more than twenty of his men, including his son. In recent years, several groups have unsuccessfully searched for the wreck, including the Quest Corporation and the *Glomar Explorer* in 1975.

SAN SABASTIAN (SEBASTAN)

Englishman George Compton's pirate ship chased the Spanish ship *San Sabastian* in the Outer Santa Barbara Channel. The *San Sabastian* hit a rock reportedly about two miles off the northeast point of Santa Catalina Island and sank in about 170 feet of water on January 7, 1754. It was said to have carried about $2 million in treasure heading for Manila, Philippines. Another story indicated that it sank halfway between Santa Catalina and San Clemente Island in the Outer Santa Barbara Channel. Twenty-one crewmen and passengers survived the shipwreck, but the pirates captured, tortured and reportedly killed the survivors. This wreck was probably salvaged over time.

SANTA CATALINA ISLAND TREASURES
More than fifteen pounds of gold in several leather pouches were found by a treasure hunter on Santa Catalina Island. A Mission San Juan Capistrano treasure was said to have been hidden in 1833 at Santa Catalina Island. See MISSION SAN JUAN CAPISTRANO TREASURES, Orange County.

SANTA CECILIA
The Spanish frigate *Santa Cecilia* sank in 1852 with supposedly $1.2 to $2 million in gold off the northwest point of Santa Catalina Island off Ship Rock, which is about one mile north of Isthmus Cove.

SANTA DOMINGO
This Spanish galleon sank in 1540 in the South Channel Islands.

SANTA MARTA
After a four-month voyage from the Philippines, the Manila galleon *Santa Marta* grounded on Santa Catalina Island in 1582. The ship reportedly carried about two hundred tons of cargo containing porcelain, gold and other Pacific Islands goods. The passengers and crew survived and made it to shore. In 1583, a Spanish salvage group from Acapulco went to salvage the ship's cargo. Some treasure could remain.

SANTA ROSA
This Spanish galleon sank in 1717 in the South Channel Islands.

SHIPWRECK TREASURE
In the Northridge area, a legend claimed that shipwrecked Spaniards buried a chest of coins. The Reseda Boulevard and Eddy Avenue region was a location mentioned.

SIGNAL HILL TREASURES

Signal Hill has a number of lost treasure stories. They could all be variations of the same story or just a few different stories. A Spanish treasure worth $3 million was reportedly buried in the Signal Hill area. See DON JUAN'S GOLD, Los Angeles County. A Mexican group reportedly buried their treasure near Signal Hill and didn't return to retrieve it. Indians supposedly attacked and killed a mining party near Signal Hill. The miners reportedly buried their gold nearby. Near Signal Hill, $125,000 in gold bullion was also reportedly buried.

SPILBERG PIRATE TREASURE

The Dutch pirate Spilberg reportedly hid pearls on the Boca de Santa Monica Ranch, a few miles north of Santa Monica, in about 1817.

MADERA COUNTY

GERMAN MINER'S GOLD

See Merced County.

JIM SAVAGE'S CACHE

See El Dorado County.

MARIN COUNTY

DRAKE MARIN COUNTY TREASURE

In 1579, Sir Francis Drake was rumored to have hidden Spanish gold, silver and gems in the San Francisco Bay area. Three bronze teapots were recovered in Drakes Bay by a dragline near Point Reyes and could have been part of Drake's booty or from the *San Augustin* shipwreck. Drake and his crew spent five weeks in Drakes Bay careening and repairing his ship and resupplying for the voyage home to England. The *Golden Hind* carried about thirty-five (or forty) tons of silver and gold, which were unloaded and stored in a fort. In some stories, fearing that the *Golden Hind* would be overloaded with treasure, part of the Spanish loot was buried in the area. See DRAKE TREASURE, Monterey County, and *GOLDEN HIND* TREASURE, San Luis Obispo County.

Sir Francis Drake, the English pirate who looted Spanish ships and reportedly hid some of his treasure in California. *Library of Congress.*

FARALLON ISLANDS WRECK
Northwest of the Farallon Islands, a Spanish galleon supposedly sank.

RANCHO BURDELL TREASURE
Chief Camillo Ynitia of the Olompali Indian tribe sold off the Olompali Rancho for $5,200. He reportedly buried the money in or near a Rancho

Burdell building before his brother murdered him. The cache was reportedly never found.

San Augustin

Four Manila galleons set sail from the Philippines for Acapulco, Mexico, on July 5, 1595. The *San Augustin*'s Portuguese captain, Sebastian Rodrigues Cermeno, had commanded the Spanish galleon *Santa Ana* in 1587, which pirates captured and plundered. The *San Augustin* was a three-masted, eighty-foot-long, 200-ton galleon carrying 130 tons of silks, spices, porcelains, a small amount of gold and silver ornaments, ivory, jade and ebony. Legends claim that the *San Augustin* carried $500,000 worth of jewels, ivory, gold and porcelains. The other three Manila galleons sailed to Acapulco, while the *San Augustin* took a different course to reach and explore the Alta California coast and then sail south to Acapulco. The Spanish Casa de Contractacion ordered captains and navigators to chart new lands as they sailed the oceans.

The *San Augustin* sighted land near Cape Mendocino and sailed south for three days before anchoring in a bay about thirty miles north of San Francisco on November 6, 1595. Most of the crew got into a small boat and went ashore, where they were greeted by friendly Miwok Indians eager to trade.

A severe storm from the southwest hit in late November 1595, when only ten crewmen were aboard the *San Augustin*. The storm caused the *San Augustin* to drag its anchors and run aground on rocks off Point Reyes. The ship sank, with a priest and at least one crewman dying. Some of the ship's cargo was salvaged by local Miwok Indians. The ship's survivors sailed a small boat south along the Alta California and Baja California coast. They reached Chacala, Mexico, on January 31, 1596, after traveling two thousand miles. The *San Augustin*'s survivors brought news of the discovery of the great natural harbor of San Francisco Bay, which they had found on San Francisco's Day.

In 1596, four Spanish ships sailed up the coast to salvage the *San Augustin*. Very little was recovered by the salvage expedition since the *San Augustin* had been scattered by storms and currents. Local Miwok Indians had salvaged part of the cargo.

Hundreds of fragments of Chinese porcelain dishes and bowls, as well as bottle glass, have been recovered by archaeologists in shell midden excavations of area Miwok villages. In 1941, a Japanese iron spearhead was recovered from a local Indian midden. Chinese porcelain still washes ashore from time to time from the wreck. Treasure hunter Robert Marx found musket balls and Ming Dynasty porcelain shards from the *San Augustin*. A dragline recovered three bronze teapots in 1961 that could have come from the *San Augustin*.

In 1982, 1983, 1997 and 1998, the National Park Service conducted remote underwater sensing in the Point Reyes National Seashore looking for the *San Augustin*. In the early 1990s, Robert Marx thought that he found the *San Augustin*. The *San Augustin* may be located in both the Point Reyes National Seashore and the Greater Farallones National Marine Sanctuary.

Tennessee

On March 6, 1853, during the gold rush, the 1,275-ton sidewheel steamer *Tennessee*, with 551 passengers aboard, passed through a fog and storm going to San Francisco. It was dashed onto rocks in what is now called Tennessee Cove. Fourteen chests of gold were salvaged. All the passengers got ashore. The wreck is on the southern part of the beach.

Mariposa County

Frenchman's Gold

A Frenchman on Maxwell's Creek near Coulterville had a smelter. He reportedly buried a pot full of gold in the basement or walls of his mill or in the area. A falling timber at his mill killed him.

Gold pan containing large gold nuggets. *Library of Congress.*

JOAQUIN MURIETTA MERCED RIVER GOLD

Another Joaquin Murietta gold coins cache was said to be hidden near Hornitos. Another variation has $60,000 in gold cached near the Merced River in a cave near Bagby (Benton Mills). The cave supposedly contained skeletons as well.

LOST CAVE OF ESCONDIDO MINE

This lost mine was supposedly located close to Bagby on the Merced River. A few burro loads of gold were said to have been hidden in Cave Escondido by a Mexican miner. He returned home to get help from friends and family to mine more gold but was killed; his gold was never recovered.

LOST SIERRA RICA MINE

This is said to be only three to five miles from Midpines.

MOUNT OPHIR MINT COINS

John L. Moffat owned a mine and an assay firm that minted octagon-shaped fifty-dollar gold coins in the 1850s. He established a mint on the edge of Mariposa. Some of his employees were thought to have buried a cache of the rare coins in the area.

MOUNT OPHIR MINT GOLD

On December 12, 1851, Mariposa County treasurer and tax collector Joseph F. Marr was said to have had three hundred unique fifty-dollar gold slugs minted at the Mount Ophir Mint with him. He tried to ford flooded Bear Creek or Dead Man's Creek to return to the Mariposa County seat of Aqua Fria on current California Highway 49. Marr and his horse drowned

A miner's rock cabin in Mariposa County in 1934. Miners hid their pokes of gold and coins in and around their cabins. *National Park Service.*

while attempting to cross the creek between Mariposa and LeGrand while heading for the Lewis Store. Marr's body was recovered about two miles below the crossing. When the water receded, the tax collector's dead horse carrying empty saddlebags was discovered on a gravel bar about one mile below the crossing. Miners and others looked for the lost gold coins. No one reported finding any coins. Several theories were suggested about why the gold coins disappeared. Marr may have thrown the gold off the horse to lighten it when he had trouble crossing the flooded creek. Another theory was that he buried the gold near Bear Creek before attempting to cross the creek. It could also be that someone found the gold coins but never told anyone. Marr was also have supposed to have cached gold near his cabin.

Schneider Treasure
A cache of gold coins was reportedly buried at Bear Valley Mountain.

Snelling Stagecoach Loot
Near Snelling, gold coins from a Sonora stagecoach robbery were reportedly cached.

Wah Chang's Gold
Rich Chinese merchant Wah Chang had a business in Coulterville where he stored about $75,000 in gold from various mines to ship out for refining. The night before it was to be transported, robbers stole the gold and murdered Wah Chang. Some believe that his gold was cached nearby.

Mendocino County

Mendocino Shipwreck Gold
A legend claimed that a ship carrying $65,000 in gold bullion from Alaska sank near Mendocino. The ship's captain reportedly removed the safe from the ship and buried it ashore.

Outlaws Gold Cache
In Russian Gulch, north of Mendocino, outlaws reportedly cached more than $65,000 from a stagecoach robbery.

MERCED COUNTY

GERMAN MINER'S GOLD
A successful German gold miner (One-Eyed Gus) supposedly cached $10,000 in gold (several burro loads) on Sherlock Creek, a few miles from the Merced River, a few miles above Bagby. He got supplies at a store on the Merced River and headed for his mining claim up rain-swollen Sherlock Creek during a storm and vanished. It was thought that he drowned. This treasure may be located in Madera County.

JIM SAVAGE'S CACHE
See El Dorado County.

JOAQUIN MURIETTA SNELLING LOST LOOT
Joaquin Murietta reportedly raided Mokelumne River and Calaveras River mining camps and then camped near Snelling on the Merced River. A legend claimed that the gang buried $30,000 in gold near this camp. In the 1930s, there was a report that a dredge brought up a chest but that it fell back into the river.

PROSPECTORS' CACHE
Three successful prospectors in 1857 supposedly had $15,000 in Mt. Ophir Mint $50 gold pieces and $180,000 in gold when they camped on the Merced River near Snelling while heading for San Francisco from the mines. It was thought that they hid their gold before going to sleep. Gunshots were heard by inhabitants in nearby Snelling during the night. When the camp was investigated, it was discovered that the three prospectors had been murdered in the night, and their horses and gear were taken by the murderers. No one reportedly found their gold. Some presumed that the robbers did not get it, but it is likely they did.

SOTO'S LOST LOOT
Outlaw Juan Soto was a member of Tiburcio Vásquez's gang who had a hideout in the Saucelitos Valley west of Rancho Panoche San Juan y Los Carrisalitos, where he supposedly hid his share of the ill-gotten spoils. Soto was gunned down by Santa Clara county sheriff Henry Morse at a fiesta.

STAGECOACH STRONGBOX

A strongbox from a stagecoach robbery around 1855 was reportedly cached near Snelling. The robber was killed in a fight but reportedly gave poor directions to his loot's location. Some believe that it may be covered by gold dredge tailings.

MODOC COUNTY

CAPTAIN DICK'S GOLD NUGGETS

Indian Captain Holden Dick found gold nuggets from possibly Pine Canyon in the Warner Mountains or near Patterson Lake in the southern Warner Mountains. Another possible location was near Owl Creek and Pine Valley northeast of Eagleville.

Some thought that the nuggets might have been from the Lost Cement Mine. He traded his gold for supplies in Alturas. Captain Dick killed two claim jumpers and then was murdered. While Captain Dick worked his mine, a sheepherder supposedly discovered him and the mine. The sheepherder claimed that Captain Dick put a flat rock over the mine entrance to hide it. After Captain Dick's murder (or hanging by vigilantes for killing claim jumpers), the sheepherder recovered some gold from the mine and then vanished. Captain Dick's wife also disappeared. One story indicated that the lost mine was between Pine Valley and Owl Creek. It could be in Lassen County.

LOST CEMENT MINE

There are several versions of this story, with some thinking that Modoc County is where the lost mine was. See Mono County.

MONO COUNTY

BODIE CACHE

A miner supposedly cached $25,000 near his home on the edge of Bodie. He was killed by a drunken miner. Local citizens, knowing of his cache, searched in vain for it.

Standard Gold Mill and the town of Bodie. *Library of Congress.*

BODIE STAGECOACH LOOT

A stagecoach going from Bodie to Carson City, Nevada, was reportedly robbed of $30,000 in gold bullion by two outlaws. A posse caught the robbers on a trail. They killed one outlaw and took the other to jail, where he died. The outlaw loot was thought to have been hidden about twenty miles north of Bodie on the old road from Bodie to Carson City.

LOST BODIE MINE

This was reportedly near Bridgeport.

LOST CEMENT MINE

In 1857, three German brothers (two men) were escaping from hostile Indians when they found gold in a cement-like rock and collected about ten pounds of ore samples. Before they reached San Francisco, one brother broke his leg and later died or was killed. The second brother also died. When the third brother arrived in San Francisco, he was very ill. Dr. Randall treated the remaining brother and told the man that he was dying. The ill man gave Dr. Randall a rough map of the area where they found the rich gold ore. The map reportedly showed that the ore deposit was south of Mono Lake at the Owens River headwaters in the Pumice Flat area of old lava flows. Other versions claimed that it was gold nuggets in shale, which would indicate an old river channel like the channels found in the Mother Lode.

In the spring of 1861, Dr. Randall arrived at Monoville, where he hired two men to take him to Pumice Flat, some eight miles north of Mammoth Canyon. Dr. Randall staked out a 160-acre claim later known as Whiteman's camp, recorded the claim and returned to San Francisco.

In the summer of 1861, a man known as Farnsworth came to Monoville and reportedly found a rich cement-like ore south of Mono Lake near the Owens River headwaters. San Franciscan Robert Hume carried $700 when he went with Farnsworth a few days later and left Monoville. A few weeks later, Farnsworth returned to Monoville, claiming that he and Hume had been attacked by hostile Indians, who killed Hume. Farnsworth insisted that he had bullet holes in his coat, but Monoville's citizens thought that the bullet holes were knife holes so they put Farnsworth under guard. A search committee of local citizens followed a trail to a small creek about four miles northeast of Pumice Flat where Dr. Randall's 160 acres was located.

The creek later became known as Deadman Creek after the committee discovered a campsite and followed one man's tracks to Deadman Creek and a pile of rocks. Under the rocks was Roger Hume's head. His headless body was found nearby and was identified by a ring on his finger. Farnsworth escaped from jail a few days later while the guard was asleep.

In the spring of 1862, Dr. Randall returned to Monoville. He hired eleven men, including a cook named Van Horn and miner named Gideon "Gid" F. Whiteman. Dr. Randall showed the men the ore from the German he treated and told the story of the lost mine. He had his employees search the 160 acres for the lost ledge, but a few weeks later, Dr. Randall vanished. Only Whiteman stayed to look for the lost mine, using Monoville as his base of exploration. Rumors claimed that Whiteman killed Dr. Randall for the gold. Whiteman also disappeared. One story variation indicated that Whiteman looked for the mine until he died in 1883.

Van Horn and two others supposedly found something, but Paiute chief Joaquin Jim chased them off the site. Van Horn became sick in San Francisco, and his two partners left for the mine, never returning. Van Horn told a friend the story of his partners and the mine. Two men, Kirkpatrick and Colt, went to Monoville to search for Van Horn's partners. Later, two skeletons were discovered at a campsite that were thought to be the remains of the partners Kirkpatrick and Colt.

In San Francisco in 1877, a dying man named McDougall claimed he worked for a man named Kent who found Dr. Randall's mine in 1869. Kent and McDougall mined the site and supposedly sent $400,000 worth of ore to Chicago before they halted mining in 1877; they hid their mine and left. The man called Kent may have been Farnsworth. Kent also vanished. Over the centuries, a number of people prospecting for the Lost Cement Mine have mysteriously died or disappeared.

LOST DESERTERS' MINE
Two of General John C. Frémont's soldiers were camped about five miles west of Bridgeport when they reportedly found a rich gold deposit. They deserted the army and mined the gold. They were eventually arrested for desertion and sent off. They reportedly never made it back to their mine.

LOST DOGTOWN MINE
This was said to be within three miles of Bridgeport.

LOST ILL MINER'S LEDGE
A miner had a gold mine in the High Sierra north of Mono Lake. He took ill and came to the nearby camp of his friend Shephard, who took him to a Carson City, Nevada hospital. The ill miner wanted Shephard to take over his mine, but the ill miner died before he could give directions to the mine.

LOST SONORA PASS LEDGE
A Mexican (Spanish) mining party reportedly found a rich gold ledge in the later 1840s near the peak of Summit Pass. They had an *arrastra* near Sonora. Indians attacked and killed all the miners, so their ledge was lost. The east slope of Sonora Pass area and north of the old Pass Road has been mentioned as a possible location. This could be in Alpine County or Tuolumne County.

LOST STRAY MULE MINE
A Mexican man chasing his stray mule stumbled on a rich gold deposit west of Mono Lake in the High Sierra. He and a partner sold four mule loads of gold before Indians killed them and the mine was lost.

MURDERER'S GOLD
In 1862, a gambler named Keyes supposedly buried seven large pickle bottles of gold dust under a tent that served as Mart Taylor's "free and easy" place in Monoville. Afterward, Keyes murdered a man and was sentenced to San Quinton Prison for life.

Sheepherders' Lost Rocks

Two Indian sheepherders coming down from pastures in the fall with their sheep and gear from the McGee Creek area west of Crowly Lake picked up some rocks to balance their mule packs. When the sheepherders unloaded the mule packs, a prospector, George Brown, saw the rocks and told them that one of the rocks was rich gold ore. Brown and the sheepherders looked in vain for where the rock came from.

Monterey County

Aztec Treasure

A treasure map reportedly found in a Canadian monastery supposedly disclosed where the Aztecs had hidden part of their vast treasure when Cortez conquered the Aztec empire in 1521. The site was said to be near where Mission San Antonio was now located on Fort Hunter Liggett, an old U.S. military base. Reportedly, a treasure hunter drilled a hole at the site indicated on the map and found a tunnel. He was unable to excavate, so he left and never returned. To date, no Aztec treasure has been found on the military base. Archaeological surveys have found no indication of Aztecs or Aztec treasure.

Cortez meeting Montezuma. Montezuma ordered the Aztecs to hide much of their gold, possibly in California. *Library of Congress.*

CARMEL MINE SHAFTS
Near Carmel in March 1940, cave-ins of old mine shafts appeared. Many believed that these cave-ins were old mines operated by Mission San Carlos Borromeo de Monterey padres.

CONE PEAK PADRE MINE
A lost padre mine was supposedly located below Cone Peak. An earthquake-caused landslide may have covered the mine entrance.

DON SANCHEZ'S TREASURE
Don Jose Sanchez's wife's brother, Jerry Mahon, knew where Don Jose Maria Sanchez hid his life savings—seventeen sacks, each with $5,000 in gold dust. Don Sanchez was an *alcalde* and rancher at San Juan Batista who had supposedly drowned. His estate administrator reportedly found the sacks of gold and moved Don Sanchez's gold to the administrator's house, where he demanded a large sum of money to release it to the heirs. Don Sanchez's wife remarried, and there were legal battles, kidnapping and murder involved over the treasure. Finally, Jerry Mahon hid the treasure but was killed in a gunfight at a hotel in Monterey. The vast amount of gold may be in the Monterey area or possibly in San Benito County.

DRAKE TREASURE
In 1579, English pirate Sir Francis Drake's ship the *Golden Hind* sailed along the California coast in 1579 looking for a Spanish Manila galleon. Drake left England in December 1577 with a commission and financing from Queen Elizabeth I and others. His mission was to steal Spanish treasure and hunt for the legendary Northwest Passage. Drake successfully plundered Spanish ships and towns but never found the Northwest Passage. Drake and his crew supposedly cached treasure from the Spanish galleon *Nuestra Senora de la Concepcion* (called *Cacafuego* or *Spitfire*) and other raids near Monterey. Stillwater Cove, near Carmel's famous Pebble Beach, was a likely area for his cached loot. Drake named California New Albion, but the name didn't stick. See DRAKE MARIN COUNTY TREASURE, Marin County, and *GOLDEN HIND* TREASURE, San Luis Obispo County.

INDIAN CARMEL SILVER MINES
An Indian supposedly worked a mine near Carmel and sold his silver ore in Carmel. He took different routes to prevent being followed to his mine. Another story was that another Indian had a mine only about two hours by foot from Monterey.

Mission Carmel was the base for several Santa Lucia Mountains Spanish lost mines. *Library of Congress*.

LOST MISSION CARMEL MINE/LOST PADRE MINE

The Lost Mission Carmel Mine or Lost Padre Mine was supposedly near Point Lobos and inland in the Santa Lucia Mountains. Spanish soldiers forced Indians to work the mine. These Indian miners were reportedly murdered when the soldiers left for Spain. When young M.J. White reportedly visited Mission San Luis Obispo de Tolosa in the 1870s, an Irish priest related a story of an Indian chief who donated a large piece of silver ore to the padres that was smelted into a crude silver cross. In the 1870s, the silver cross was still at the mission.

The Indian chief led the padres to a three-foot-wide silver deposit in the Santa Lucia Mountains. The padres mined the silver until Indian uprisings caused them to abandon the mine. A crude cross was supposedly located near the mine entrance. A map showing the mine location was said to have been lost when a messenger with the map drowned in a flooding stream while heading to Mexico City. A plague later killed two padres who knew the mine's location.

M.J. White, his friend Pedro and White's dog went hunting up Santa Margarita Road and took a trail for a high country lake. White shot and wounded a buck deer. They tracked the wounded animal into a deep mountain canyon, where they stumbled across a narrow foot trail cut into the side of the canyon walls. They found man-made rock debris piles as well as a tree-cleared area. They discovered an old mine with a rotting timber cross outside the mine entrance.

The boys collected an ore sample and tethered their horses in a flat area next to a spring. They tracked down the dead buck deer and packed it up. A mountain lion came by that night, so they built large fires in their camp and near their horses to discourage the predator. High winds came and spread the campfire sparks to surrounding trees and brush. The old mine's timbers caught fire, and the mine collapsed. The two boys and their dog fled the raging fire. After two days, they reached the coastal town of Cayuca. The rock sample they brought along with them from the mine contained rich silver ore. White and Pedro were never able to find the area, as the fire changed the landscape. White's story may be a tall tale, as he did not reveal it until 1903.

In 1893, many mining claims were filed in the southern Santa Lucia Mountains in areas once controlled by Mission San Miguel de Archangel. Miners found a large mine dump near a mine, as well as an *arrastra* with granite blocks near a stream. The mine had caved in. The miners recovered ore samples that reportedly had high silver content, with some gold.

Lost Mission San Antonio De Padua Priest Mine

This silver mine was associated Mission San Antonio de Padua. Before the Spanish arrived, Indians reportedly mined a mineral deposit. The mined silver ore was reportedly refined at Mission San Antonio de Padua. This lost mine was in a rugged area. A portion of the trail to the mine was high enough that the travelers could see the ocean. The mine was abandoned about 1833 when the padres were expelled and many missions were shut down by the revolutionary Mexican government.

In 1948, two men filed mining claims on what may have been the Lost Priest Mine. Abandoned old mining equipment was at the site. The Jolon Mining District in the Santa Lucia Mountains is near Mission San Antonio de Padua. From around 1850 to at least 1870, placer gold was mined in the Jolon Mining District. Another site could be north of San Simeon in the Dutra Creek area.

Lost Valley Mine

While chasing Indians, Spanish soldiers supposedly found a mine in Lost Valley. They forced the Indians to mine it. Eventually, the Indians had enough and revolted. They overcame the Spaniards and hid the mine. Human bones, Spanish coins, armor and weapons have been uncovered over the years in Lost Valley.

Lost Ventana Mine

Mission San Carlos Borromeo del Rio Carmel was founded in 1770 on the beautiful Carmel Peninsula. Only a day's walk southeast of Mission Carmel, the mission's Ventana Mine was located in the Santa Lucia Mountains. Reportedly, the Ventana Mine was visible from the mission's bell tower. The Indian miners were also able to see Mission Carmel's bell tower from the mine's entrance. Thus the mine was called Ventana, which means window in Spanish. Another legend claimed that Indians gathered yellow sand and nuggets from a cave about a day's walk from the 4,853-foot-tall Ventana Double Cone, which are two mountain peaks that appear to form almost a window, which could be another reason for the mine's name. The mine may be located in the Ventana Primitive Area southeast of Monterey. Los Burros Mining District is in this area, so this story appears to be likely.

Mexican Treasure Ship

A legend claimed that a Mexican ship with a $9 million (current value) treasure of gold and silver with jewels and supplies sailed for Monterey. On the approach to Monterey Bay, pirates attacked and sank the ship. Captain Barstow in 1908 or 1909 found a wreck he believed was this treasure ship, but he never seems to have recovered any treasure. I could find no historic evidence on this treasure ship.

Mission Carmel Treasure

In 1818, when pirate Hippolyte de Bouchard raided Monterey, the Mission Carmel padres reportedly put most the mission's religious treasures in a deerskin sack, which was then hidden in the Santa Lucia Mountains under a large oak tree by a trusted blind Indian and his friends. The pirates bypassed Mission Carmel after they sacked and burned Monterey after a battle with a shore battery. Bouchard's ships then sailed south to Santa Barbara. When the padres asked the Indian to recover the Mission Carmel treasure, he supposedly couldn't locate the right trail and oak tree. After digging under many oak trees in the mountains, they reportedly gave up the search.

Above: The Spanish battery site overlooking Monterey. Bouchard's pirate ship *Santa Rosa* was disabled around here. *Author's collection.*

Left: Mission San Antonio de Padua in about 1890. At least one lost padre mine was nearby. *Library of Congress.*

MISSION SAN ANTONIO DE PADUA TREASURE

Mission San Antonio de Padua was built in 1771 and reportedly sold a large number of horses for about $50,000 in gold in the 1800s. A legend indicated that some mission Indians and one soldier left the mission bound for a small ship in a harbor on the coast to transport the treasure from California. The gold and the party mysteriously disappeared. They were said to have been ambushed by robbers. Along Willow Creek in the Santa Lucia Mountains, a few old Spanish coins have been recovered. This could have been part of the missing mission treasure.

Point Lobos Gold

Mission Carmel Indians reportedly recovered gold flakes from black sand washed into a sea cave near Point Lobos. They could enter the cave only when the water was low, which was when there was an extremely low tide and calm sea. The cave was underneath a cliff, which reportedly collapsed in the 1940s. The source of the gold washing into the Pacific Ocean may be nearby.

Rich Silver Ore

In 1802, Ignacio Ortega retrieved an ore sample from a mineral deposit in the Santa Lucia Mountains not far from Monterey. The sample came from a mineral vein opposite the King's Ranch, northwest toward Serrita. A mining expert recovered six ounces of silver from the ore, which indicated rich silver deposits in the area.

Vásquez and Rancher Pinnacles Treasures

See San Benito County.

Will H. Martin Treasure Found

Will H. Martin buried caches of gold coins on his property in Monterey about 1900. In 1948, during the construction of a school at the site of Martin's former home, about $6,000 in face value gold coins were uncovered, with about three hundred people searching for his caches. One twelve-year-old boy, Mike Malarasa, found a can with $740 in $20 gold pieces at the site. This story was carried in many newspapers.

Napa County

Napa Stage Loot

Near Napa, gold coins from a Napa stagecoach robbery were reportedly cached.

Payroll Cache

In 1888, a stagecoach was robbed south of Middletown just north of the Napa County line. The strongbox, with more than $2,000 payroll inside, was supposedly buried near the Calistoga-Middletown stage route (California Highway 29) or the Ida-Clayton Toll Road. This could be southwest of Middletown or north of the Sonoma County line. This could also be in Lake County or Sonoma County.

Nevada County

Donner Party Treasures

The Donner Party of emigrants had winter camps at several sites west of present Truckee, California. They were traveling to California's Sacramento Valley when winter snows blocked the pass. The Donner Party's Alder Creek camps contained two tents and a lean-to separated several hundred yards from one another near Alder Creek. About twenty-five people inhabited the Alder Creek Camps, including twelve children, during the winter of 1846–47. George Donner; his wife, Tamsen; their five children; and Doris Wolfinger resided in one tent, along with Jacob Donner, Elizabeth Donner, their five children and two of Elizabeth's children from a former marriage. Solomon Hook and William Hook occupied another tent. The Donner family's eight employees were in the lean-to across Alder Creek from the tents.

The Donners sold their farm of about one quarter section of land in Springfield, Illinois, for $10,000 before they headed in wagons for California. Most Donner money was sewn into a quilt in their big wagon. Individual family members also carried money belts. The Donner family owned five wagons of possessions, as well as commercial dry goods to sell in California. The Donner family left Missouri very late in the season. They waited too long to cross what is now known as Donner Pass over the towering Sierra Nevada Mountains. A member of the Donner Party, Luke Halloran, was twenty-five years old when he died of a lung disease around August 26, 1846, in what is now Utah. Halloran left the Donners his $1,500 in gold and silver. Tremendous snows in November 1846 forced the emigrants to camp at what is now called Donner Lake (formerly Truckee Lake) for the winter. There was also a camp at the site of Donner State Park. The Graves Cabin was located in Truckee north of current Interstate 80, near where a school now stands.

The Donner family may have hidden their money at or near their Alder Creek camps. One legend also claimed that some of treasure may have been cached in Utah on the Hasting Cutoff. George Donner, at the age of sixty-two, died of blood poisoning from a chisel cut accident. Jacob Donner, his wife and some of their children all died during the winter. About December 16, 1846, in the Alder Creek camps, Jacob Donner and three teamsters died and were eaten by the survivors. Tamsen Donner later offered members of one of the relief parties $500 in cash to carry her kids to safety. On March 26, 1847, while near death, forty-five-year-old Tamsen Donner trudged to Lewis Keseberg's cabin to ask for help. Tamsen Donner's husband, George

Top: Donner Pass Pioneer Monument, where twenty-two feet of snow trapped emigrants. Passes like this were often associated with lost emigrant and robbery treasures. *Author's collection.*

Bottom: This Alder Creek meadow was near a Donner Party camp that may contain lost treasure. *Author's collection.*

Donner, had just died. Lewis Keseberg was in the cabin, where he survived off the remains of five people who had died in the cabin. Keseberg claimed that Tamsen Donner told him she had hidden the Donner family's money in her tent. Keseberg promised her that he would retrieve the treasure to later give to her children. Tamsen Donner died that night in Keseberg's cabin, and Keseberg feasted on her body. There were always suggestions that Keseberg murdered the desperate Tamsen Donner and others to become food for his survival.

Keseberg said that he went to the Alder Creek camps and claimed he found only $531 in gold and silver. He said that he kept the gold and cached the silver at the bottom of a pine tree.

On April 17, 1847, the Fallon rescue party reached the Alder Creek camps. They searched for survivors and the Donners' money. To rescue the

Donner Party survivors, the rescue party had been promised $3 per day for normal travel and $5 per day when going through snow. Members of the party threatened to kill Lewis Keseberg if he did not give them the Donner family's money and seemed more interested in salvaging goods and getting cash than rescuing the few remaining survivors. Keseberg reluctantly turned over $225 in gold that he hid in his waistcoat. Keseberg pointed to a spot under the limb of a large tree where Fallon party members George Tucker and John Rhoads dug up a cache of $273 in silver. The rescue party had a contract with *alcalde* John Sinclair, allowing them half of any recovered Donner Party money and goods. Eliza P. Donner Houghton, who was a young girl when she was trapped with her family, didn't have any information on her family's missing money when she later wrote a book, *The Expedition of the Donner Party and Its Tragic Fate*, on her and the Donner Party's ordeals.

Archaeological excavations since the mid-1990s in the Tahoe National Forest have recovered a number of scattered artifacts, including an 1839 British coin, which may have come from the Donner Party Alder Creek camps. It is believed that the British coin from the Isle of Man was owned by John Denton, a British-born teamster in the Donner Party. The Donner Alder Creek camps may be under the Prosser Creek Reservoir, which includes part of Alder Creek and Prosser Creek. The Alder Creek camps could be in the Tahoe National Forest or on adjacent private land.

There is a possibility that Lewis Keseberg found and buried the Donner family money and did not disclose this to the Fallon relief party. German Lewis Keseberg was smart, well-educated, spoke four languages and did

Prosser Creek Reservoir may cover some of the Donner Party's unfound treasure. *Author's collection.*

whatever it took for him to survive. Keseberg settled down in Sacramento, where he was tried for murder for his actions in the winter of 1846–47, but under the circumstances, he was not convicted of murder.

Keseberg worked for Swiss businessman John Sutter, who controlled his empire from Sutter's Fort near Sacramento. John Sutter employed smart men as emigrants flooded into California's Central Valley and the Sierra Nevada Mountains during the gold rush started at his mill on the American River. Keseberg found opportunity by opening a boardinghouse and then the Lady Adams Hotel in 1851 in Sacramento. He had a number of businesses during the California Gold Rush. In 1851, Keseberg's hotel burned down. His Phoenix Brewery, which he was about to sell for $50,000, was destroyed in the Sacramento flood of 1861–62. Keseberg became destitute. He could have used recovered Donner family money to fund his commercial enterprises. Forty-two members of the Donner Party died, and forty-eight survived the horrible winter of 1846–47 in the Sierra Nevada Mountains between Sacramento and Reno, Nevada.

Elizabeth Graves's Donner Party Treasure Found

Sierra Nevada miner Edward Reynolds was part of a Donner Lake fishing party when he wandered off looking for quartz on the upper end of Donner Lake on May 14, 1891. Reynolds discovered old coins on the ground about four hundred feet from Donner Lake. He immediately picked up $10 in coins. His friend Amos Lane joined him, and they recovered 117 U.S. dollars (1806–44), 74 half dollars (1813–43), 48 Mexican dollars (1826–45), one Spanish dollar, one Bolivian dollar (dated 1836), a La Plata dollar (dated 1835), five Saxony marks (dated 1835), 51 five-franc pieces (1806–44) and two Spanish half dollars (1800 and 1805). The coins were Donner Party member Elizabeth Graves's cache. She hid $300 to $500 during the severe winter of 1846–47.

Elizabeth Graves's wagon carried the coins to California hidden in auger holes bored in cleats nailed to her wagon bed to hold a table inside her wagon. William McCutchen, a member of one of the Donner Party rescue parties, had helped a starving Elizabeth Graves remove the money from its hiding place. Some members of the rescue party joked about playing a card game to see who would get her money. Ill and nearly dead, she hid her money near Donner Lake the next morning on March 4, 1847, before attempting to cross over the mountains with the rescue party. During the trip to the Sacramento Valley, Elizabeth Graves died and was cannibalized by the surviving rescue party members.

In 1891, a fishing party on Donner Lake found Elizabeth Grave's lost treasure. *Author's collection.*

Reynolds and Lane later gave the coins to Elizabeth Graves's descendants. Many newspapers at the time carried the story of the found treasure. Some of the Graves children had used the coins to teethe on so they had teeth marks on them. Since she reportedly had much more money, she may have hidden it in another cache or some of it may have been found by others and not reported.

HINES LOST GOLD
In 1897, Hines supposedly hid thirty pounds of gold in Strawberry Valley.

LAKE VERA LOST GOLD CACHE
Close to Lake Vera or the Lake Vera Lodge, a miner cached his gold near his cabin before going to Nevada City and disappearing.

LOST FRENCHMAN MINE
This is thought to be located near Grizzly Hill in Frenchman's Canyon, not far from Nevada City.

Mayberry Treasure
Near the mining camp of Bloody Run, miner Mayberry supposedly cached about $40,000 in gold. Mayberry wouldn't tell robbers where he hid his gold, so they murdered him.

Nevada City Lost Padre Mine
A Lost Padre Mine was reportedly in the Nevada City area. Nevada City had many deep-shaft gold mines, including the rich Empire Mine. Any lost padre mine near Nevada City would likely have been found and mined. This area contained some of the richest gold deposits in the United States. The Empire Mine State Historical Park is located in Nevada City.

Strongbox Loot
In 1856, between Nevada City and the Sacramento Wharf, outlaws were said to have robbed a stagecoach of about $27,000 in two strongboxes. Some thought the loot was cached a few miles from Nevada City.

Orange County

Irvine Ranch Gold
A legend indicated that about $30,000 in gold bars was taken from a strongbox during an 1868 robbery of the Los Angeles to Santa Ana stagecoach. Five bandits robbed the stage near Carona del Mar. A posse from Santa Ana stumbled on the robbers camped near the robbery site and killed all five. The stolen gold was not reportedly found. It was hidden somewhere on the ninety-three-thousand-acre Irvine Ranch, which includes the current city of Irvine.

Mission San Juan Capistrano Treasures
On November 1, 1776, Padre Junípero Serra established the present Mission San Juan Capistrano. Pirates under French Captain Hippolyte de Bouchard—260 men in the thirty-eight-gun frigate *Argentina* and 100 men in the twenty-six-gun *Santa Rosa*—anchored off Dana Point on December 16, 1818. Captain de Bouchard put ashore 140 men with two cannons to sack the Spanish town and Mission San Juan Capistrano. They were met on shore by 30 soldiers from the Presidio of San Diego who had been dispatched to oppose their landing. De Bouchard's men had just sacked the Spanish

capital of Alta California, Monterey, as well as Santa Cruz, Rancho de Rufio and Santa Barbara up the California coast.

San Juan Capistrano's citizens and padres hid their treasure and fled inland. The Spanish soldiers had a brief skirmish with the pirates before the Spanish soldiers also fled inland. About $100,000 in gold coins supposedly was buried near Mission San Juan Capistrano. Three Americans and one Englishman deserted from the pirates to the Spaniards. Much treasure supposedly remained hidden due to the revolutions in Mexico against Spain that followed. In 1821, Mexico separated from Spain. Later, the Mexico revolutionaries expelled the padres from Mission San Juan Capistrano. Mission San Juan Capistrano's treasure was supposedly cached in Trabuco Canyon. See TRABUCO CANYON MINE AND TREASURES, San Diego County.

Sometime after 1900, a Hermosillo, Mexico priest reportedly traveled to San Juan Capistrano and used a treasure map to hunt for the mission's treasure. However, the treasure location markers were missing or altered. The priest never found the treasure. Mission treasure supposedly was also hidden by mission Indians east of Santa Anna. Another mission treasure may have been buried on Santa Catalina Island. See SANTA CATALINA ISLAND TREASURES, Los Angeles County.

OLD MISSION SAN JUAN CAPISTRANO TREASURE
On October 30, 1775, Padre Fermín Lasuén established the first Mission San Juan Capistrano on the San Juan River. When Indians revolted and attacked Mission San Diego de Alcalá, the Mission San Juan Capistrano padres reportedly buried their mission's bells and fled to the safety of the Presidio of San Diego. Also, a treasure supposedly was cached at the first Mission San Juan Capistrano site near the San Juan River. The padres and the Christian Indians may also have transported church treasure to the nearby hills and buried it during their escape to the Presidio of San Diego. Almost one year later, the padres returned, dug up the mission bells and established a new mission at the present site of the Mission San Juan Capistrano, about five miles from the original site. Since 1859, the old mission grounds have been dug up by treasure hunters.

TRABUCO CANYON MINE AND TREASURE
Legends indicated that Mission San Juan Capistrano had several abandoned and hidden Spanish mines in the mountains. One mine was reportedly in the area of Trabuco Canyon. A treasure was also supposedly cached in Trabuco Canyon during the 1818 Bouchard pirate raid. Due to a land dispute between

the Nieto family and the mission padres, treasure was supposed to have been hidden nearby. Fearing that the new Mexican government would confiscate their mission treasure, three keys were said to have been attached to a tree as the markers to find the padres' cached treasure. A man named Marelino was said to have found three keys that had fallen off an ancient tree limb. Marelino took the keys to the mission, but none knew their significance until later. Trabuco Canyon contains the Trabuco Mining District, where small amounts of placer gold have been found. See MISSION SAN JUAN CAPISTRANO TREASURE, Orange County.

PLACER COUNTY

LOST IOWA HILL MINE
This was supposed to have been close to the headwaters of the East Fork of the American River.

Hydraulic mining near French Corral. *Library of Congress.*

A group of gold miners working their claim on a creek in the mountains. *Library of Congress.*

LOST YANKEE JIM MINE

In 1848, a Maine sailor jumped ship, as did hundreds of other sailors, to go to the gold fields. He was known as Yankee Jim and traded chunks of gold for gold coins when most miners were just finding gold nuggets and gold dust. His mine was said to have been near a gold mining camp that became known as Yankee Jim. Yankee Jim vanished, and his mine was supposedly between the East Fork of the American River and the Middle Fork of the American River. One article thought that he may have been mistakenly hanged in 1852 as a horse thief, even though he had hunks of gold in his money belt.

MOUNTAINEER ROADHOUSE CACHES

The Mountaineer Roadhouse was an outlaw haven for Tom Bell and other outlaws during the gold rush days. The Mountaineer Roadhouse was on Folsom Road almost three miles from Auburn and thirty-six miles northeast of Sacramento. Several outlaw caches were reportedly hidden nearby. This site may be under the waters of Folsom Lake.

STAGE ROBBERS LOOT

Robbers were said to have cached loot from a stagecoach robbery in the hills between Auburn and Forest Hill.

PLUMAS COUNTY

HONEY LAKE TREASURE

Successful French gold miner Henry Gordier established a cattle ranch in 1857 on Baxter Creek, near the north shore of Honey Lake, not far from present U.S. Highway 395 and Janesville. Gordier disappeared in early 1858 when three strangers took over his ranch. They claimed that they purchased his ranch and that he returned to France. The neighbors noticed that the strangers were digging holes all over the ranch. The neighbors believed the strangers had likely murdered Gordier and were looking for his cache of about $40,000 in gold coins and nuggets. They formed a vigilante group and captured the three. Under interrogation, the three men claimed that they knew nothing about any gold on the ranch. Soon thereafter, Henry Gordier's body was discovered in the Susan River near its junction with Willow Creek. After Gordier's body was found, the three men were hanged by the vigilantes. In 1877, Mary Dunn and others found a cache of several gold nuggets and a gold coin that may have been from Gordier's cache. One big gold nugget was worth $240 at that time, when gold prices were probably about $21 per ounce. Gold was not found naturally in this area, so someone had to have moved the gold nuggets there. This could be in Lassen County.

LOST LEDGE OF GOLD

A prospector in the fall of 1850 reportedly found a rich brownish ledge of gold about fourteen inches above ground. The prospector marked nearby trees so he could return to mine the ledge in the spring. When spring arrived, he couldn't find the site. After looking for it for a number of years, he gave up the search. It was thought that a forest fire and time had hidden his ledge.

MARKS'S GOLDEN STREAM

A prospector called Marks and his partner searched for a remote stream containing gold that a friendly Indian had told them about. Marks's partner became ill, so Marks looked for it alone. Marks found the stream, but hostile Indians drove him from the site. Marks returned to Marysville and told his tale. About thirty prospectors followed him up into the mountains to mine the stream in force. The group reportedly went east up Last Chance, Humbug and Red Clover Valleys and then west to where Nelson Creek joined the Upper Feather River. With their food running low, the group broke up, and many thought they were on a wild goose chase. Some thought that the stream was near Camel Peak and was later found near Rich Bar.

PERALTA MINE
See Calaveras County.

RIVERSIDE COUNTY

BAKING SODA CAN CACHE
An emigrant family reportedly buried their savings in a baking soda can near Marble Canyon and the Colorado River.

JUAN CHAVEZ CACHE
Juan Chavez was associated with Joaquin Murietta's robberies in northern Mexico. Returning to California, Juan Chavez was in charge of a mule train reportedly carrying $200,000 in gold. When they stopped in a canyon, a lone guard was left to watch the mule train and treasure while the others rested. The guard led the mules off and reportedly hid the gold near a tree. After he returned, he was confronted by Juan Chavez and murdered. The mule train continued a ways before the gold was found to be missing. One location associated with the cache is near Sage.

LOST HUNGARIAN PLACER MINE
This lost placer mine was reportedly in a rocky gulch east on Baseline Road beyond the New Dale Mine.

LOST PAPUAN GOLD MINE
Papago Indian Papuan was survivor of Apache attacks and moved from western Arizona to join a Mohave Indian band with his wife. The band traded $75,000 worth of gold from their mine near the southern part of the McCoy Mountains. In 1886, Apaches killed Papuan. In 1906, a man named Hartman tried to get Papuan's wife to show him the secret mine location, but she refused.

LOST PEGLEG SMITH MINE
Thomas L. "Pegleg" Smith and a partner called Le Duc crossed Colorado River at Yuma Crossing bound for Los Angeles in 1828 or 1829. While looking for water, Smith climbed to the top of a butte that was yellow at the bottom and black on top. He picked up black nuggets rich in gold and continued on his way. Some think that this lost mine is in the

Chuckwalla Mountains near Guilliday Well. Another location was said to be the tallest of three cone-shaped buttes between San Bernardino and the Chocolate Mountains.

LOST SCHWARTZ MINE
In 1899, prospector Nicholas Schwartz supposedly found $18,000 in gold nuggets in lower Rock Horse Canyon. He put a rock over the mine entrance and left but never returned. He gave his friend a roughly drawn map of the site but refused to guide him there. Another version of the story has Schwartz and his Indian wife getting $70,000 worth of gold from the mine in a year, going to San Francisco and then disappearing. A number of people claim to have found the mine but no gold.

LOST YACAIPA SPANISH GOLD MINE
See San Bernardino County.

LOUIS RUBIDOUX'S CACHE
See San Bernardino County.

MORENO OUTLAW CACHE
See San Bernardino County.

MURIETTA RAWSON CANYON LOST LOOT
Joaquin Murietta and his gang (or Chavez) reportedly stashed loot ($212,000 or $200,000) in Rawson Canyon near a cross engraved tree (or oak tree). Rawson Canyon is about 8.5 miles south of Hemet.

WILEY WELLS STAGE STATION CACHES
Near the Wiley Wells Stagecoach Station west of Blythe, several outlaw caches were supposedly hidden.

SACRAMENTO COUNTY

LOST WELLS FARGO CHEST
On the bank of the Sacramento River near Sacramento, a Wells Fargo chest full of gold was supposedly stashed in the 1850s.

TOM BELL FOLSOM CACHE
Outlaw Tom Bell reportedly cached some of his loot near Folsom.

WASHOE'S LOST GOLD
The 385-ton (or 500-ton) steamship *Washoe* was built in 1863 at San Francisco. The *Washoe*'s boilers overheated and blew up on September 4 or 5, 1864, in Steamboat Slough above an island called the Hog's Back in the Sacramento River Delta. The explosion and sinking killed sixteen whites and a score of Chinese people. Several more died out of the thirty-six people seriously injured. The *Washoe*'s crew reportedly took a large amount of gold from the *Washoe* and cached it on the bank of Steamboat Slough. The *Washoe* was raised a few months later and continued cruising the Sacramento River.

SAN BENITO COUNTY

DON SANCHEZ'S TREASURE
See Monterey County.

LOST PADRE GAVILAN RANGE SILVER MINE
A legend claimed that the Lost Padre Silver Mine was in the Gavilan Range near Hollister. Fremont Peak, formerly called Gavilan Peak, was named after John C. Frémont and is 3,173 feet high. It is part of Fremont State Park. Mission San Borromeo del Rio Carmel Indians reportedly mined there, with silver tailings reportedly found in this area.

TOM SING'S TREASURE
Bandits robbed Chinese merchant Tom Sing's iron safe of a reported $780,000 in gold in 1875. A posse quickly caught up with the bandits and hanged them. The missing gold was evidently cached along the Salinas River somewhere.

VÁSQUEZ AND RANCHER PINNACLES TREASURES
Another of outlaw Tiburcio Vásquez's treasures was reportedly cached near Hollister and the area of the Pinnacles National Monument. Two rock faces, Tiburcio's X and Vásquez's Monolith, are named after a legend that he hid in a cave there. He may have left behind as much as $500,000 worth of treasure. A rancher was also rumored to have cached his wealth near the Pinnacles. This could be in Monterey County.

San Bernardino County

Alvord's Lost Gold

Charles Alvord discovered gold in the Mohave Desert in 1860. Several areas were said to contain Alvord's lost ledge of gold in black manganese. Alvord had been looking for the Lost Pegleg Smith Mine or the Lost Gunsight Mine. Areas mentioned as possible locations for Alvord's gold ore are Mule Spring, about twenty miles north of Manix in the Owl-Hole region, northeast of Yerimo; Butte Valley in the Panamint Range; Happy Canyon and Spanish Canyon in the Alvords; and about fifteen miles northeast of Mount Acron near Bitter Spring. The Alvord Mine on maps is not this lost mine. Several expeditions hunted for this lost mine over the years without success.

Avawatz Mountain's Gold

The Avawatz Mountains are in Death Valley National Monument and Fort Irwin Military Reservation. A Mormon found chunks of rock along an emigrant trail. He used the rocks to encourage his tired mules to keep pulling his wagon in the Death Valley Desert. He put some of the rocks in his pocket and later found them to be gold bearing when he examined them. Another story was that Bob Blade found gold quartz float from a ledge, but storms changed the landscape and he couldn't find the ledge.

Barstow Hobo Gold

A hobo reportedly broke into a freight car and found gold bars inside. The train supposedly stopped near a horse corral and group of trees near Barstow. The hobo got out of the freight car and hid some of the gold bars before getting back on the train and leaving the area. One gold bar was reportedly found in the area.

Bernarr Macfadden Cache

Wealthy publisher Bernarr (born Barnard) Macfadden owned the Arrowhead Springs Hotel. He was known to hide money in various places. One of his wives wrote a book, *Barefoot in Eden*, detailing where she found his caches. She did not find any at Arrowhead Springs. He was an eccentric publisher of pulp fiction and healthy living magazines.

Bullion Mountains Gold

Ed Shaw lost a gold ledge in the Bullion Mountains foothills, some fifty miles southeast from Draggott. A chimney-shaped black butte in the Bullion

Mountains towered above black gold nuggets with possible sulfur powder deposits nearby.

CALICO GAMBLER'S CACHE

A gambler named Pat Hogan reportedly buried $20,000 three feet from a big rock in Wall Street Canyon near Calico. Pat Hogan and his partner, Wong Lee, were shot by the owner of Lucky Joe's Gambling Palace for winning too much. Wong Lee died, but Pat Hogan survived and left Calico. Hogan was later killed in a fight in Las Vegas, Nevada.

DON TIBURCIO TAPIA TREASURES

See Los Angeles County.

KOKOWEEF MOUNTAIN'S RIVER OF GOLD

Kokoweef Mountain is located south of I-15 and southwest of Nipton. Kokoweef Mountain's gold story was started by prospector E.P. Dorr, who signed an affidavit on November 16, 1934, regarding his visit to fantastic caverns there. This affidavit was published in the *California Mining Journal* issue of November 1940 and has caused quite a stir since then. There are several versions of this complicated story. The bottom line is that no huge amount of gold has been recovered from the site. The cave entrance was dynamited and caved in. Several explorers died in the cave in 1959. Numerous articles have been written about this story. Two Paiute Indians were said to have found a caved-in tunnel with underground water and gold in black sand. One Indian drowned, and the other Indian never returned to the site. It was also called Crystal Cave. Mining companies have been involved on the site for years but have found no gold in spite of excavating many tunnels.

LOST ARCH MINE/ARCH DIGGINGS

There are at least two versions and locations of this mine. A group of Mexican miners claimed to have found a rich gold strike and recovered more than $30,000 in gold before leaving. In about 1883, Amsden and another prospector reportedly left Needles for the Turtle Mountains. Amsden arrived in Goffs after wandering incoherent, fatigued, starving and dehydrated. His partner had died. Amsden claimed that he found a deposit of gold scattered in the desert. The site had a natural stone arch as a marker. A tub of gold nuggets was supposedly buried and recovered. One location could be in the Old Woman Mountains, with three peaks grouped together, with one of them looking like a hat. Another location was near the Turtle Mountain

Road to the southwest near a black lava hill and a ways off California Highway 95. This may be twenty-five miles north of Rice on the north slope of Turtle Mountain. People have searched for more than a century for it. One writer thought that the site was off I-15 northeast of Baker.

Lost Bull Ring Mine
A French miner had a rich mine whose entrance he covered with brush and boards with a bull ring attached. It was said to be near Mule Springs in the Black Hills some fifteen miles west of the Colorado River. Another possible location was fifteen miles south of the Vallecito Stage Station.

Lost Burro Ledge of Gold
During the night, a miner's burro wandered away from his camp. The miner searched for it in the Kelso Mountains. The miner stumbled across a ledge of gold and took a few samples before he continued searching for his lost burro. It became dark and the miner got lost. Eventually, he made it back to civilization without ever finding his burro. He was also unable to locate the ledge of gold-bearing rock.

Lost Dutch Oven Mine
This is likely a made-up story about a lost mine in the Clipper Mountains west of Danby. A writer in 1953 interviewed the alleged source of the story, Tom Schoefield (or Scofield or Schofield), who discounted the story of the lost mine and Dutch oven full of gold nuggets.

Lost Gunsight Mine
See Inyo County.

Lost Lee Mine
Old man Lee was a prospector who frequented San Bernardino to get supplies. He found a rich mine and hired a hand to help cut a shaft. He returned to San Bernardino to get supplies, as his worker was about out of food. He sold bullion and left but was later found murdered a few miles east of San Bernardino. His murder was a mystery, as he still had his watch and money. A group from San Bernardino set out to find Lee's missing worker and maybe the rich mine. Neither was found. Some think that the mine was in the Bullion Mountains and may be in the U.S. Marine base. Another site may be north of Old Woman's Well in the San Bernardino Mountains.

LOST MOHAVE MINE

The Hualapai and Mojave Indians reportedly had a secret mine. Miner George Nay in 1892 claimed that he followed an Indian trail in the southwestern Mohave Mountains across the Colorado River from Topock, Arizona. He lost his way and couldn't relocate the lost mine after he found it.

LOST MORMON MINE AND TREASURE

A lost Mormon mine and treasure were said to be in the Clipper Mountains, which are south of I-40 and southwest of Fenner in the Mohave Trails National Monument. In 1866, Adams and a group of Mormons mined on the north side of the Clipper Mountains northeast of Essex. They supposedly hid their gold under the floor of their cabin near the mine. Indians attacked and killed all but one or two miners. Rancher Beet Smith may have stumbled onto the site after being thrown from his horse. He found rich ore and an old mine shaft but never could find the site again.

LOST SHEEP HOLE MINE

Supposedly, in the northwest portion of the Sheep Hole Mountains near Amboy, L.O. Long and his partner found a rich placer mine. Long's partner became ill, went to San Francisco and later died. Long continued working the mine but got injured and made his way to San Bernardino after caching his shotgun and other items near the mine. On his deathbed, Long wrote a letter indicating that the mine was about fifteen miles west of the south end of a dry lakebed. It was supposed to be near a stream in a brushy canyon. Some think that the dry lake was Bristol Dry Lake, which is southeast of Amboy.

LOST YACAIPA SPANISH GOLD MINE

In the Yucaipa area, another lost Spanish gold mine was said to have been hidden. Indians told Mission San Gabriel padres about the gold mine. This could be in Riverside County.

LOST VAN DUZEN CANYON MINE

Prospector Van Duzen and his partner reportedly had a mine in Van Duzen Canyon between Big Bear Valley and Holcomb Valley in 1860. It was also said to be between Gold Mountain and Bertha Park in Holcomb Valley. Van Duzen and his partner were found murdered in their cabin. Another man in 1868 claimed that his partner had found the mine but never had any proof. This man also lost the mine's location and looked for the mine without any luck.

Louis Rubidoux's Cache
North of Riverside, rancher Louis Rubidoux owned Rancho Jurupa and San Temoteo Rancho, which covered about thirty-two thousand acres in the 1850s. It had a gristmill and winery. Rubidoux was said to have buried a chest of gold near the Agua Mansa Cemetery in the Rattlesnake Mountains due to Indian and outlaw attacks in the area. One site mentioned was in the southern part of Slovet Mountain south of Colton. The flood of 1862 was said to have wiped him out. This could be in Riverside County.

Moreno Outlaw Cache
In San Goronio (now Beaumont), the Bradshaw Route stagecoach office was reportedly robbed of $20,000 in gold coins in the 1880s by a gang of four or five. The gang crossed the Moreno Badlands and camped in some mesquite near Moreno. A posse caught up with them the next morning, and all were killed. No gold was found, so it was thought they lightened their horses by caching their loot somewhere. This could be in Riverside County.

Robbers Needles Cache
Two bank robbers in the early 1930s held up a Needles bank. Their car broke down north of Victorville and Oro Grande near the Mohave River. They were quickly captured, but the loot was not with them. Both went to prison, where one died in an escape attempt; the other died in prison.

Spanish Carreta Treasure
See Kern County.

Spanish Fort Treasure
Near an old Spanish fort on Big Lake a few miles above Fawnskin, a large amount of gold was said to have been hidden. There doesn't appear to have ever been a Spanish fort in the area. A gold rush did occur in this area in 1860.

SAN DIEGO COUNTY

Bigamist Caches
James P. "Bluebird" Watson married rich women and took their money. He reportedly murdered fourteen of his twenty-five wives and hid maybe

$200,000 in one or more caches in the Borrego Desert. He was convicted of murder and died in San Quentin Prison of tuberculosis in 1939.

CAPITANA SHIPWRECK
Off Panama's Pacific coast, a small Spanish fleet's *capitana* under General Juan de Velasco lost its rudder during a storm in 1600. The Spanish fleet had been on a trading and exploration trip in the South Seas. It was also hunting for a Dutch fleet. The rudderless ship drifted and reportedly wrecked possibly somewhere north of San Diego. One potential wreck site may be near the point in the Cabrillo National Monument. In 1973, several old Spanish coins were recovered from a beach at Cabrillo National Monument.

CHURCH TREASURE
See Imperial County.

CONFEDERATE GOLD
During the Civil War, a party of Confederate sympathizers heading to enlist in the Confederate army supposedly transported $50,000 in gold for the Confederacy. They were said to have been ambushed on the Emigrant Trail above Agua Caliente by Union forces and supposedly cached their gold in the area. The *Official Records* reported that near Agua Caliente on November 29, 1861, a party of Confederate sympathizers led by a man named Showalker was captured by part of the Union First California Cavalry Regiment. Since the Showalker group was bound for Texas through a route through Sonora, Mexico, there may be some truth in gold being buried in the area.

CORTEZ BANK WRECK
In about 1701, a Spanish galleon supposedly carrying $700,000 to $1 million in gold and silver wrecked off the Cortez Bank.

CORTEZ TREASURE
The Cortez Treasure was said to have been cached in Oceanside near Mission San Luis Rey de Francia, which was established in 1798.

JESUS ARRORA TREASURE
In 1682 off San Diego, Jesus Arrora's pirate ship was reportedly wrecked. The surviving shipwrecked pirates ended up at Sheep Head Mountain just south of Mount Laguna. The survivors lived off the land and found some placer gold. Pirate Jesus Arrora may have placed a note in a metal chest with

gold nuggets and buried it below a crude cross. Indians attacked and killed Arrora and all his pirates. A Spanish prospector found a cross in 1873 but didn't find any buried chest or gold nuggets.

LOST BLACK CROW MINE

Dutchman Dietz hunted for the Lost Peg Leg Mine in northern Blair Valley. He became ill and was found in the desert. He was hospitalized and couldn't remember where he found the rich gold ore that he carried out of the mountains. All he could remember was that it was near a cave and that a black crow flew over the area.

LOST EL CAJON MINE/LOST INDIAN MINE/LOST BARONA MINE/LOST WADHAM MINE/LOST EL CAPITAN MINE

El Cajon Mine was said to be near El Capitan Mountain. Mission San Diego de Alcalá's religious ornaments were said to have been cast from El Cajon Mine silver. A Mission San Diego de Alcalá padre supposedly met a young Indian boy playing with a quartz arrowhead containing gold streaks. When asked where the arrowhead came from, the boy replied that

A typical small mining facility. *Library of Congress.*

it came from a village near El Cajon. When the padres went to the village, the Indian chief told the padres that the nearby mountains contained much rock like the boy's arrowhead. The padres convinced the chief to keep the gold deposit's location secret. The Indians mined the gold ore and supposedly took several bags of gold ore each month to the mission. The padres refined the gold and sent it to their church headquarters in Mexico City. They also made gold ornaments and decorations.

In 1833, the revolutionary Mexican government expelled the padres who hid El Cajon Mine. Through the years, El Cajon Mine became also known as the Lost Indian Mine, Lost Wadham Mine, Lost Frenchman Mine and Lost Barona Mine. Padre Jose Barona was a friar at the San Diego de Alcalá Mission, so it could be named after him or after the Barona Mission Indians, who now have a reservation and casino in the area. Wadham owned the Barona Ranch at one time. Instead of one mine, there could be several lost mines in the same area. Some stories indicate that it was a gold mine, while others claim that it was a silver mine.

Pierre Hausenberger was a Frenchman called Don Pedro. Don Pedro supposedly transported sacks of silver from the lost El Cajon Mine to San Francisco in 1854. After he disappeared, his lost mine was called the Lost Frenchman Mine.

An Indian's adobe hut looked down the Barona Valley on the north slope of El Cajon Mountain. In 1875, the Indian living there reportedly took three mule loads of silver to Los Angeles and sold them to a Sonora Town silversmith. The Indian drank too much, so outlaws robbed and killed him. Many prospectors searched unsuccessfully in the area near the Indian's hut for the Lost Indian Mine.

In about 1900, a prospector researched the lost mine by talking to the Mexican silversmith who had purchased silver ore from the Indian. He led some prospectors to the Indian's adobe hut, tore it apart and found several smelted baseball-sized to coconut-sized silver chunks.

Thomas Y. Gillingham prospected Black Mountain, about fifteen miles north of El Cajon Mountain. Reportedly, he had seen Spanish documents from Mission San Luis Rey de Francia claiming that a large amount of silver ornaments had been made from mined El Cajon silver. Gillingham discovered an old trail leading to the Indian's hut near El Cajon and found a small spring. He recovered about twenty pieces of native silver, about 87 percent pure silver, from a few ounces to ten pounds in weight. Five Indians appeared in Gillingham's camp and said the padres put a curse on the old mine and that he should leave.

In the Barona Valley, he headed north and located a caved-in mine entrance. Removing the mining debris, he discovered a small room cut into the mountain and recovered about two hundred pounds of refined silver in the storage room. He removed more refined silver, which he sold for about $6,000 in Los Angeles. Gillingham later prospected in the Mojave Desert and Colorado Desert, where he also had success.

Gillingham then bought an orchard. By 1905, several Indians were also known to have sold some silver from the El Cajon area. Indian Juan Valdez worked for Gillingham. Valdez told Gillingham a story about his grandfather Jesus (Soos) Moreno, a mission Indian at Mission San Diego de Alcalá. Moreno had talked to a man called Don Pedro about an old Spanish mine and showed him its location. The padres' curse on the mine affected Don Pedro and Juan Valdez's father. Juan Valdez's father took Juan Valdez to a spot above a spring and pointed to the mine location, but Juan Valdez had never visited the mine.

In 1906, Juan Valdez agreed to help Gillingham look for the mine. During their trip to the mine, Valdez refused to go farther and disappeared. Gillingham then spent a week alone looking for the mine entrance. He later discovered that Juan Valdez's family had left two days after Gillingham and Valdez left for El Cajon. Gillingham later retired to San Diego and died in 1948 without finding the lost mine.

LOST SCHWARTZ MINE
See Riverside County.

MADRE DE DIOS
The Spanish galleon *Madre de Dios* supposedly wrecked off present Carlsbad, about two miles south of Oceanside and about thirteen miles north of Solano Beach. A legend claimed that $150,000 in treasure was salvaged from the wreck. This ship is not in the State Lands Commission shipwreck list, so it may be a legend.

MISSION SAN DIEGO DE ALCALÁ GOLD
Padre Junípero Serra established Mission San Diego de Alcalá on July 16, 1769, as the first permanent Spanish settlement in Alta California. This first San Diego mission was located on Presidio Hill overlooking Mission Bay in the present city of San Diego. Mission San Diego de Alcalá prospered and controlled the area of nearby Indian villages. The Presidio of San Diego was built near the mission to protect Spaniards from hostile Indians. Due to

The Padre Serra Monument in Monterey, where Serra established a mission linked to lost mines and treasure. *Author's collection.*

conflicts between Presidio soldiers and mission Indians, Mission San Diego de Alcalá moved in August 1774 to a hill farther from the presidio.

The padres supposedly used mission Indians to mine precious metals from the mountains. The padres were said to have hidden a gold altar and gold in a large wooden chest in a hole in a Poway Valley canyon.

In 1775, two Indian neophytes, Zegotay and Francisco, escaped from Spanish mission lands. Spanish soldiers chased the two Indian neophytes to force them to return to work on mission lands.

Spanish soldiers on El Camino Real, traveling from San Diego to Presidio Monterey with mail, grazed their horses near the road in a field of Indian crops. This was one more act that caused the Indians to want to drive the Spaniards from their lands. Zegotay and Francisco were in a nearby Indian village and urged the Indians to revolt against the Spanish oppression.

About eight hundred neophyte and gentile (or unconverted) Kumeyaay Indians from nearby Indian villages attacked Mission San Diego de Alcalá after midnight on November 4, 1775. There were only eleven Spaniards—including three soldiers, Padre Luis Jaymes (Juyme), Padre Vicente Fuster, two blacksmiths and two boys (Lieutenant Ortega's son and nephew) in the mission.

Upon waking, the Spaniards fled to the mission's adobe powder magazine, which contained arms and ammunition. Since they had muskets, the Spaniards were able to defend against the attackers, who had only bows and arrows, clubs and spears. Padre Luis Jaymes went out to confront the attacking Indians, proclaiming, "Love God, my Children." The Indians dragged Padre Jaymes from the mission grounds and killed him. The mission blacksmith and a carpenter were also killed, as were several hostile Indians. The Indians looted the mission and burned down most of the mission buildings. Spanish troops from Presidio of San Diego arrived and rescued the Spanish mission survivors. The mission was rebuilt eight months after the attack.

In 1833, the Franciscan padres were expelled from California, so they supposedly hid their silver mines in the Coastal Range and treasure. At Black Mountain, some trusted mission Indians supposedly hid a chest with church ornaments in a crevice and put a flat rock over the crevice or in a mine shaft.

Mission San Diego de Alcalá had a dam, tunnel and aqueduct from a creek as its water supply. The water tunnel was reportedly a hiding place of the padres' treasure. A silver mine near Starvation Peak, west of Ramona, was another rumored treasure location.

Left: Classic view of the bells of Mission San Diego de Alcalá. *Author's collection.*

Right: Mission San Diego de Alcalá reportedly had several lost mines and hidden treasures. *Author's collection.*

Mission San Diego de Alcalá is about five miles east of I-5, near I-8 in Mission Valley. See Lost El Cajon Mine/Lost Indian Mine/Lost Barona Mine/Lost Wadham Mine/Lost El Capitan Mine and Trabuco Canyon Mine and Treasure, San Diego County.

Mission Santa Maria Treasure

An Indian legend claimed that gold, silver and church treasure from an Arizona mine and mission were hidden in a cave or in an old Spanish silver mine maybe near Ramona for movement to San Diego. Spanish symbols on trees and rocks were made to help locate the treasure. One version of the legend has two ox carts of gold and church treasure (including silver candlesticks) hidden in about 1833 when the padres were ordered from Mexico. The treasure was to have been put onboard a Spanish ship for shipment to Spain. The treasure cave or silver mine was reportedly sealed with an iron door hidden by stones and debris. The Indians returned to Arizona, and the padres who hid the treasure were reportedly killed by hostile Indians.

Mission Santa Ysabel Treasures

In 1818, Mission Santa Ysabel was established as part of Mission San Diego de Alcalá's missionary network. It was located about sixty miles east of San

Diego as a temporary chapel and became a sub-mission (*aristencia*). In 1821, it was upgraded as a permanent mission in the Santa Ysabel Valley for some 250 neophytes. Around 1822, more than 450 neophytes were attached to Mission San Ysabel. The mission was located about seven to nine miles north of Julian in San Ysabel. In 1924, near the junction of California Highway 78 and California Highway 79, a new chapel was built.

The mission's two silver or bronze bells were purchased by the local mission Indians for six burro loads of barley and wheat. One bell was made in 1723. The second bell had "San Pedro 1767" cast in it. In 1926, the two church bells were stolen. Some believed that they were cached nearby. Another tale has one bell cut up to be sold for scrap and the other cached in the Big Sur area. The top of one bell was returned to the mission and was in the mission's museum.

A legend indicated that the mission's Spanish padres buried four hundred gold and silver ingots near Mission Santa Ysabel when they were expelled in 1833. Another tale has the mission treasure cached at a pass between San Diego and Santa Ysabel when the padres were attacked. Their cache may have been above the San Felipe Valley Butterfield Stage Station and might have consisted of gold and silver coins. Another potential cache site was below the San Ysabel Mission altar. A version of this tale has the cache marked by three stones with a cross visible on the stones from the old chapel dormitory. Several mission padres reportedly died when they fled the country.

Mule Loads of Gold

Indians were said to have attacked a party carrying several mule loads of gold in saddlebags going from Mission San Diego de Alcalá to a Los Angeles mission. The gold was reportedly hidden in caves in canyons north of San Diego.

Murietta Carizzo Hill Cache

Another of bandit Joaquin Murietta's caches was supposedly near Carizzo Hill not far from Mission San Luis Rey de Francia.

San Jose

On June 16, 1769, the Spanish galleon *San Jose* sailed from San Blas, Mexico, carrying food, fine vestments and three bells intended for the Spanish missions at San Diego and Monterey. Storms hit the *San Jose* and broke its foremast. Winds and currents forced the *San Jose* 750 miles southeast to

Puerto Escondido. The *San Jose* was repaired at Puerto Escondido and tried to resume its journey north in May 1770. It was never heard from again. It may have sunk off Southern California in the San Diego area or off Baja California, Mexico.

Santa Rosa and *Bishop*

On October 3, 1717, the Spanish ship *Santa Rosa* hit a fifteen-foot-deep reef off Bishop Rock in the south southeast part of Cortez Bank and sank. The *Santa Rosa* reportedly carried a cargo of $700,000 in gold and silver. Bishop Rock is southwest of San Clamente Island. Bishop Rock got its name in 1855 (1877 on State Lands Commission list) when the clipper ship *Bishop* hit the rock and also sank.

Santo (Santa) Domingo

In 1540, the Spanish ship *Santo Domingo* reportedly sank about five miles off the mouth of Escondido Creek in the South Channel Islands. The *Santo Domingo* supposedly carried $3 million in gold bullion and silver specie. This is the same time period as the *Trinidad*, detailed as follows.

Stagecoach Carrizo Loot

See Imperial County.

Treasure Canyon Trove

An abandoned stage station (Vallecito or Vallecitos) supposedly had bandit gold hidden three miles northeast of the stage station in Treasure Canyon.

Trinidad Treasure

Three Spanish caravels, including the thirty-five-ton *Trinidad*, sailed in 1539 under Captain Francisco de Ulloa from Acapulco to explore and search for the Seven Cities of Cibola. A Spanish land expedition led by Francisco Coronado also searched for the Seven Cities of Cibola and traveled through the current states of Arizona, Kansas, New Mexico, Oklahoma and Texas.

De Ulloa had been part of Cortez's army that conquered Mexico. The caravel *Santo Thomas* was scuttled off present Caliacan, Mexico. The caravel *Santa Agueda* returned to Acapulco after discovering that Baja California was a peninsula and not an island. From De Ulloa's travels, part of the Gulf of California was named the Sea of Cortez.

The following story is taken from Oceanside ophthalmologist, amateur archaeologist and writer Dr. Joseph Markey. His story was widely disputed by historians and reporters, as no evidence was ever presented for most of his claims. Dr. Markey claimed that De Ulloa died in 1540 and was buried in California. Old trial documents show that De Ulloa was still alive in 1542.

The *Trinidad* contained twenty-four crewmen, a scribe named Pablo Hernandez and five women. Looking for an inland passage, the *Trinidad* sailed to the mouth of the San Luis Rey River and went to the Channel Islands and then back to the mouth of the San Luis Rey River. The *Trinidad* anchored at what became San Diego. Since the crew was terribly sick with scurvy, most went ashore to recover. On August 21, 1540, Pablo Salvador Hernandez and two crewmen stayed aboard the vessel. De Ulloa reportedly took coins from a chest and established a camp on the shore of a lake in an Indian village of about five hundred people. The Spaniards traded jewelry for food and other items.

De Ulloa had Pablo Hernandez bury coins about two leagues from a new camp located near some petroglyphs, which had rocks stacked around it to form a primitive fort. The scribe returned to the *Trinidad*. A three-day storm hit, and the scribe Hernandez returned ashore and found De Ulloa and the remaining Spanish party dead, except for one badly ill Mexican woman they killed to put her out of her misery. De Ulloa supposedly was buried on September 14, 1540, on a hillside amid large boulders. The other dead were put in a cave sealed by boulders.

The three Spaniards abandoned the anchored ship, got into its longboat and rowed south. One crewman died on the return trip, but Hernandez and the other crewman rowed to Acapulco. The unmanned *Trinidad* was thought to have been wrecked somewhere on the California coast. According to Dr. Markey, Hernandez returned to Spain in 1542 and died there in 1571.

Near Oceanside, a farmer found a skull in a dry lakebed that Dr. Joseph Markey claimed was about four hundred years old, making it one of the first Europeans in California. Where the skull was found, Dr. Markey reportedly found parts of Spanish leather armor, a metal knife, a metal breastplate and other metal. Dr. Markey insisted that his finds were taken to Spain, where experts confirmed that they were from the early Spanish conquistador period.

In 1947, at a Paris, France dinner party, Dr. Markey claimed that he met Miguel de Ulloa, a direct descendant of Francisco de Ulloa. This De Ulloa told him the tale about the *Trinidad* and Captain Francisco de Ulloa. Dr. Markey hired researchers to document De Ulloa's expedition at the Naval Archives in Seville, Spain. Markey claimed that Pablo Hernandez's report and his map to the treasure site were from the Biblioteca Nacional. Markey said the San Luis Rey Historical Society spent about $100,000 to $150,000 researching collections in Madrid, Vienna and Mexico City.

Using Pablo Hernandez's report and map, Dr. Markey found petroglyphs and a rock fort. About five miles northeast of the rock fort, Markey said that he and his associates found the cave full of skeletons from De Ulloa's expedition. In September 1957, Dr. Markey reportedly uncovered about two thousand coins in rotting leather bags by using a metal detector. One coin dated back to 1500. The find reportedly included two-thousand-year-old Roman coins but no gold or silver coins. Information on the find was sketchy.

Dr. Markey searched for the *Trinidad* and its treasure off Oceanside. A few Spanish coins similar to those he previously found were uncovered, but the wreck was never found. Over the years, many searched for the wreck.

Legends persisted that the *Trinidad* carried $4 million to $6 million worth of coins and treasure. It supposedly sank off Point La Jolla and Solano Beach. Three rafts with thirty-five tons of ballast were floated and allowed to drift to simulate where the *Trinidad* may have drifted in September weather and tides. All rafts drifted south and sank near Point La Jolla. In the spring of 1961, a scuba diver discovered some old gold coins off the mouth of Loma Alta Creek in the 1600 block of Pacifica Street in Oceanside. Some were Roman coins. Old coins reportedly still wash ashore from time to time in this area. In the 1990s, a diver found Spanish coins nearby. There were many rumors that this wreck and its treasure had been recovered. Dr. Markey promised to publish a five-hundred-page book on the De Ulloa expedition and treasure but never did. He died in 1985. Many believe that Dr. Markey's story likely was an elaborate hoax. De Ulloa may never have reached the San Diego area. The *Trinidad* is not in the State Lands Commission shipwreck list. See DE ULLOA TREASURE, Imperial County.

VALLECITOS ROBBERY GOLD

At the Vallecitos Stage Station, several robbers stole about $60,000 (or $80,000) in gold from a stagecoach robbery in 1876. The robbers reportedly buried the gold north of the stage station before a posse caught and killed them. Another story has $65,000 in gold hidden from a robbery between the Carrizo Stage Station and the Vallecito Stage Station on the Butterfield Stage Route. The Vallecito County Park is now located on the old stage station site with a replica of the stage station.

Vásquez Escondido Canyon Treasure
The Escondido Canyon area supposedly was another cache site for outlaw Tiburcio Vásquez's treasure.

San Francisco County

Angel Island Treasures
A wealthy Mexican reportedly came to California during the gold rush. He and his Black servant buried his treasure on Angel Island. Around 1870, the servant told the story about the lost treasure but died before he could give better instructions on its location. Another Angel Island tale had pirate Martin Thierry bury his treasure before sailing away to adventure in Russia and the Pacific. Thierry died in Java. A detective later sent then San Francisco Mayor James Rolph a letter about looking for this treasure.

City of Chester
The 1,106-ton *City of Chester* sank in August 1888 about three miles west of the Golden Gate in about ninety feet of water. Rumors of a cargo of $30 million in gold bullion have been mentioned, but this is not likely.

City of Rio de Janeiro
The 5,080-ton steamer *City of Rio de Janeiro* passed through the Golden Gate before fog and treacherous currents caused it to hit rocks on February 22, 1901. The ship had sailed from Hong Kong with 87 passengers and a crew of 140. It also reportedly carried about $2 million in Chinese silver and $37,000 in gold coins in addition to its cargo of rice, silk and tea. One story claimed that the treasure aboard was worth $11 million. The manifest supposedly had only $6,765 in gold listed, and that was recovered. Only 81 survived the wreck.

Fuhrman Treasure
In 1926, Henry Fuhrman claimed that his mother and grandmother buried gold and jewelry in 1850 when they arrived at San Francisco from Mexico. They camped in a tent near Montgomery Street and California Street and buried their valuables due to their fear of being robbed. They moved to camp at a safer location. When they came back to retrieve their valuables, the area was undergoing construction of new buildings. They were unable to

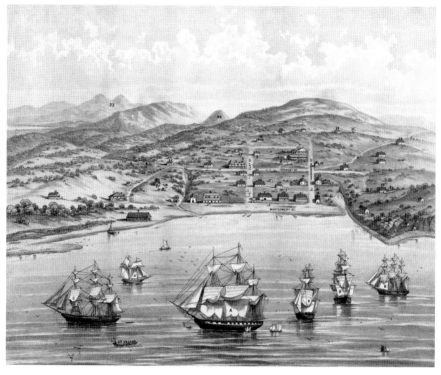

San Francisco as it was before the gold rush. It was the main entrance to the northern and central California gold fields. *New York Public Library*.

Treasure Island was a dredge-built island named for the treasure stories on adjacent Yerba Buena Island in San Francisco Bay. *Library of Congress*.

find their treasure. Henry Fuhrman came to the site in 1926 to look for their treasure when the building he thought was over the site was demolished. He claimed that the treasure was removed with the building debris.

THE *NOONDAY*'S TREASURE

The 2,100-ton clipper ship *Noonday* was carrying a small treasure from Boston, Massachusetts, when it hit a rock then called Fanny Rock, now called Noonday Rock, on the north end of the Farallon Islands on January 1 or 2, 1863. The *Noonday* went down in about forty fathoms of water. The Noonday Rock supposedly rose up one day from an earthquake. The pilot boat *Relief* from San Francisco rescued the *Noonday*'s crew and passengers.

SAMUEL S. LEWIS

The 1,104-ton screw steamer *Samuel S. Lewis* was carrying 385 passengers when it hit Duxbury Reef and sank on April 19, 1853. All aboard were rescued, so it is not likely treasure was left behind.

VALPARAISO

The sailing ship *Valparaiso* may have wrecked in the late 1870s about three miles west of the Golden Gate with $5 million in gold bullion. It may be a legend, as it is not in the State Lands Commission website shipwreck list.

YERBA BUENA ISLAND TREASURES

Yerba Buena Island is in San Francisco Bay. It was named after a wild mint found there and means "good herb" in English. The island's other name was Goat Island, due to a herd of goats grazing on the island about 1844.

In 1833, when the padres at Mission Delores in San Francisco were expelled from Mexico, they put the mission's valuables in chests to ship to Spain on a sloop in San Francisco Bay. However, a storm forced the sloop aground on the north side of rocky Yerba Buena Island. The treasure chests were supposedly unloaded onto Yerba Buena Island and buried and never recovered.

In 1837, a whaler anchored in Callao, Peru, for water and provisions. Several Peruvians saw the whaler as the chance to protect their wealth during a revolution taking place there. Four wealthy Peruvians reportedly carried two barrels containing gold and an ironbound chest containing jewelry onto the whaler for safe keeping. The whaler's captain made a deal with the wealthy men to hold their treasure for a few days until the unrest ended. They were to pay the captain for storing their treasure. The rich

Peruvians did not return to the whaler at the agreed time. The captain had his whaler sail out to sea with the Peruvians' treasures.

The whaler sailed north along the Pacific Coast and anchored in San Francisco Bay, where many whalers sought safe refuge from the often-violent storms. The whaler's boat with three or four crewmen reportedly landed on Yerba Buena Island and buried the two barrels and the iron chest. Later, the crewmen who buried the treasure deserted the whaler. One deserter was killed, and the whaling ship and its captain were lost at sea. Surviving crewman West Indian Charles Stewart arrived in Yerba Buena about 1875 to recover the treasure he buried in 1837. His memory failed him, as many landmarks were gone or altered. Stewart died in 1878 and never located the treasure.

Yerba Buena Island is part of the Bay Bridge route between San Francisco and Oakland. This route goes through a tunnel at the top of Yerba Buena Island. The Bay Bridge was constructed from 1936 to 1937. Treasure Island was created from dredge material and was the site of the 1939 Golden Gate International Exposition, San Francisco's second world's fair. Treasure Island is connected to the north end of Yerba Buena Island. Treasure Island got its name from the buried treasure stories about Yerba Buena Island.

San Joaquin County

Murietta Corral Hollow Cache
Castle Rock is two miles past Corral Hollow, which is about one mile west of Tracy via the Corral Hollow Road. A legend indicated that bandit Joaquin Murietta and his gang used the area as a hideout. One of his treasures reportedly was cached nearby.

Therien's Cache
Therien (possibly a pirate) had a hunting cabin near Woodbridge just north of Lodi. He was thought to have hidden $50,000 in gold there. In 1926, his two sons used a steam shovel to excavate around the cabin looking unsuccessfully for the gold.

Tom Bell San Joaquin Loot
Another of outlaw Tom Bell's caches was supposedly secured in the 1850s east of Stockton, in a cave or hidden in the ground. This could be at or near Mercer Caverns or Moaning Cave in Tuolumne County. Another version of this story has the location near Lathrop on the San Joaquin River.

SAN LUIS OBISPO COUNTY

GOLDEN HIND TREASURE
Legends indicate that Pirate's Cove (Mallagh's Landing) was where the one-hundred-ton *Golden Hind*'s cache worth $25 million in silver ore and coins was buried by Sir Francis Drake's crew. The overloaded *Golden Hind* carried a reported thirty-five to forty tons of gold and silver from Drake's Spanish raids on the Pacific Coast. Some treasure was supposedly unloaded and hidden in 1579 near Pirate's Cove before the *Golden Hind* sailed to Drakes Bay. The *Golden Hind* was careened before returning to England. Pirate's Cove is located on Avila Bay, about seven miles south of San Luis Obispo and five miles northwest of Pismo Beach. See DRAKE MARIN COUNTY TREASURE, Marin County, and DRAKE TREASURE, Monterey County.

GOLD ORE
An English captain in 1820 got a gold quartz ore sample from the Coastal Range. Spanish Alta California governor Don Pablo Vicente de Solá's 1818 report said that the Coastal Range mountains showed indications of metal, with eight or nine marks of silver being extracted from the Ortega Mine.

HURRICANE CREEK LOST PADRE MINE
This Lost Padre Mine was rumored to be in the Hurricane Creek area northeast of Santa Maria.

MISSION SAN LUIS OBISPO DE TOLOSA TREASURES/MISSION MINE
In 1772, Padre Junípero Serra founded Mission San Luis Obispo de Tolosa. When John C. Frémont and American forces came to the area during the Mexican-American War, the mission's silver was supposedly hidden in a cave near Bishop's Peak, one of two nearby pyramid-shaped peaks. While the mission was being restored in 1906 or 1907, brothers William Herd and John Herd were tearing up an old mission floor when they found six silver bars hidden under the floor. Older Mexicans claimed that the silver came from a mine hidden in November 1846 that was located northeast of the mission.

REED TREASURE AT MISSION SAN MIGUEL ARCANGEL
In 1791, Mission San Miguel Arcangel was founded along El Camino Real. At one time, the mission and its lands supported 1,076 neophytes,

The Padre Junípero Serra statue at Capitol Park. He helped establish many California missions. *Author's collection.*

more than 10,000 cows, more than 1,000 horses and more than 8,000 sheep. In 1832, it was recorded as having 811 horses, 50 pigs, 75 mules and 42 goats.

After Mexico ended the mission system in 1833, the Franciscan padres were expelled from Mission San Miguel Arcangel. The Mexican government took over the mission, and many Indians left the area. The church and mission lands were partitioned and used for political favors.

On July 4, 1846, Englishman William Reed, Miguel Garcia and Petronilo Rios bought most of Mission San Miguel Archangel's lands, except for the church and priests' quarters, for $600 (300 pesos, or about $250 then). William Reed's wife, Maria Antonia Vallejo, was the niece of Petronilo Rios, and her father was General Mariano G. Vallejo, a California Mexican soldier and powerful politician. William Reed managed the mission property. The old mission buildings served as his home and as an inn on

El Camino Real. He raised cattle and sheep. Captain John C. Frémont's American and Bear Flag Republic army traveled past the mission during the conquest of California.

In 1848, Reed was among those successfully recovering gold during the gold rush. Reed reportedly cached his money and gold dust somewhere on the mission grounds. The nearby existing Rios-Caledonia Adobe, which was built in 1835 by Petronilo Rios when he was a corporal in a Mexican army detachment at Mission San Miguel Arcangel, could also be a burial place for wealth.

On December 4, 1848, six men stopped at Reed's inn and had dinner with William Reed, his family and his staff. These travelers were Sam Bernard (or Barnberry), Pete Raymond, U.S. Army deserter Joseph Peter Lynch, U.S. Navy deserters Peter Remer and Irishman Peter Quin from the USS *Warren* and an Indian called John from the Soledad area. Raymond and Lynch had just murdered two miners in the California gold fields and taken their gold. Raymond also had just escaped from jail. William Reed told the six men about his arrival in California, settling down, his good fortune in finding gold in the Sierra Nevada gold fields and his successful livestock business. Reed bought thirty ounces of gold from the travelers at $30 per ounce. This was a fortune in those days.

The six travelers spent the night with the Reed family and departed the next morning south down El Camino Real. They went only as far as San Marcos Creek or possibly Rancho Santa Margarita before turning back to Mission San Miguel Arcangel. The six men surprised the sleeping Reed household and brutally murdered everyone. The eleven murdered people included the Reeds' four-year-old son, Petronilo; Reed's brother-in-law, Jose Ramon Vallejo; midwife Joseta Olivera; Martin Olivera's fifteen-year-old daughter, Concepcion, and grandson; a Black cook; an Indian sheepherder; and the sheepherder's godchild. The murderers stole some money, Maria Reed's jewelry and William Reed's coat. They were unable to find Reed's cache of gold nuggets and money. The six murderers then headed south down the El Camino Real to escape.

James E. Beckwourth discovered the bodies while on his way to deliver mail and carried the horrible news to Petronilo Rios, who lived only nine miles south of the mission at Rancho el Paso de Robles, near present Templeton. Beckwourth continued with the mail to the U.S. Army post in Monterey and to its commander, Colonel Richard B. Mason. John M. Price, San Luis Obispo's *alcalde*, traveled down El Camino Real from the Stanislaus gold mines and also found the murdered bodies.

Price signed an order for the murderers' arrest, so a thirty-seven-man posse from San Luis Obispo under Cesario Latillade rode down El Camino Real after the murderers. The six murderers camped that night near Rancho El Paso de Robles, where one of Maria Reed's earrings was later found. The next night, the murderers probably camped at Corral de Piedra Rancho, about five miles south of Mission San Luis Obispo, where Indian John left the group. The five remaining men halted at Rancho Los Alamos, where they got four horses, and then camped about a mile from Santa Barbara. Proceeding some five to six miles from Santa Barbara, they arrived at the Ortega Rancho and bought some food.

About a mile from the Ortega Rancho, the vengeful posse caught up with the murderers and trapped them against steep cliffs near the top of Ortega Hill, which overlooks today's U.S. Highway 101 and the Pacific Ocean, just west of Summerland. In the fight that followed, Ramon Rodriguez killed Sam Bernard. Ramon was also killed. Peter Quin was wounded, and Pete Raymond jumped off the cliff into the ocean and drowned.

The posse recovered eighty pesos in one stocking; eighty-two pesos in another stocking; one hundred pesos, two reales in silver and one ounce of gold in a handkerchief; and one gram of gold, seven pesos and five silver reales in another handkerchief. The recovered money and gold were likely splits of the loot from four of the murderers. One of the murderers' treasure was likely lost in the fight or buried. General Vallejo, who had several family members among the murdered, later turned over the recovered loot to Ramon Rodriguez's widow for her husband's death while being a member of the posse.

The surviving murderers confessed. They were tried and convicted of murder in a civil court. U.S. Army Colonel Mason stationed at Monterey commanded Lieutenant Edward O.C. Ord to execute them. A U.S. Army firing squad executed Lynch, Remer and Quin on December 28, 1848, at Santa Barbara since they were U.S. military deserters as well as murderers.

Mission San Miguel Arcangel is still a community church, with ancient statues and paintings almost two hundred years old. A number of years ago, I attended a wedding there.

SAN MATEO COUNTY

LOST MEXICAN JUARISTA TREASURE
See Los Angeles County.

Santa Barbara County

Aliso Ranch Treasure
On the Aliso Ranch near Solvang and the Santa Ynez Mountains, Spanish church treasure from Mission Santa Ynez was supposedly cached under two oak trees with the sharp end of miner's candles driven into the trees. The treasure contained about fifteen burro loads of silver and gold coins in rawhide bags worth $300,000. A rancher reportedly removed the treasure marker, as he did not know about the hidden treasure.

Apple Orchard Cache
At the Pat Kinevan Ranch, a cache of about two hundred octagonal fifty-gold pieces was said to have been buried in an apple orchard between Santa Barbara and Los Olivos. This could have been hidden near the San Marcos Pass summit.

Cabrillo-Drake Treasure
On San Nicolas Island, there was a rumored Cabrillo-Drake treasure.

Cabrillo Treasure
While on a voyage of discovery for Spain, Portuguese navigator Juan Rodriguez Cabrillo—with two small ships, the *San Salvador* and *Victoria*—discovered Northern California. Cabrillo's expedition left La Navidad, Mexico, on June 27, 1542, to explore north of Mexico along the Pacific coastline. In October 1542, Cabrillo landed on San Miguel Island and called it La Posesion. While exploring San Miguel Island, Cabrillo fell and suffered a compound fracture in his upper arm, with the bone breaking through the skin. Cabrillo died weeks later of gangrene and was said to have been buried in a lead coffin in full armor, along with his jeweled sword.

University of California archaeologist Philip Mills Jones found a seed-grinding stone on Santa Rosa Island in 1901 with the initials JR, which could be a fragment of the burial headstone of Juan Rodriguez Cabrillo. Some claim that Cabrillo was buried on Santa Rosa Island, not San Miguel Island.

Candleholder Treasure
A legend indicated that $1.5 million ($1.25 million) in gold and silver was cached near Solvang.

CAPITANA TREASURE WRECK

In 1610, off Point Arguello and Lompoc, a Spanish *capitana* galleon reportedly carrying a cargo of a $5 million treasure may have been wrecked. This vessel is not on the State Lands Commission shipwreck list.

LOST INDIANS MINE

Two Indians reportedly brought a sack full of gold ore to Mission Santa Barbara. The padres told the Indians that the gold ore was cursed by the devil and urged them to return it to the mountains and bury it. The padres followed the Indians but lost them in the mountains. Some believe that the Indians' mine was northwest of Las Olivos near Zaca Lake.

LOST MISSION MINE/LOST PADRES MINE/LOST PADRE PLACER

See Ventura County.

RANGER PEAK TREASURE

Near Ranger Peak, a mission treasure of Spanish gold coins and church ornaments was supposedly cached.

SAN ANTONIO

The Spanish ship *San Antonio* was in Manila, Philippines, preparing to head for Acapulco, Mexico, when Chinese and the Filipinos were revolting against Spain in 1603. Many in the Philippines were said to have put their valuables on the ship for safekeeping. One story was that on the west side of San Miguel Island, the Spanish ship *San Antonio* foundered. The ship supposedly disappeared while en route to North America. This may be a phantom shipwreck, as I have found no real proof that it sank off California. It is not on the State Lands Commission shipwreck website.

SAN MARCOS PASS LOOT/SLIPPERY ROCK LOOT

Near San Marcos Pass's summit, between Santa Barbara and Los Olivos, one of Joaquin Murietta's outlaw gang reportedly hid $30,000 in gold loot from a Wells Fargo stagecoach robbery (said to have been $20 octagonal gold coins). The outlaw was killed before he could return to recover it. There were supposedly two other treasures in the area. Another version claimed that the bandit died in prison in 1901 and told his treasure story before dying. Another variation has the loot from a stagecoach heist hidden at Slippery Rock near the Cold Spring Tavern on San Marcos Pass Road.

San Miguel Island Wreck
In 1801, near the northwest tip of San Miguel Island, a Spanish Manila galleon supposedly sank with a cargo of silver bars and plate. This vessel is not on the State Lands Commission shipwreck list.

Santa Barbara Pirate Treasure
There was a legend that pirates (buccaneers) were being approached by a Spanish or Mexican warship, so the pirates hid their treasure near Santa Barbara and Arroyo Burro Beach Park or maybe near Veronica Springs.

Santa Barbara Shipwreck
Off Santa Barbara, a Spanish galleon was said to have sunk, but its crew reportedly saved its $2 million in gold and silver, which they buried in the sand dunes on the beach.

Santa Barbara Treasure
On December 8, 1818, pirate captain Hippolyte de Bouchard's ships arrived off Mission Santa Barbara after sacking Monterey. Many Santa Barbara inhabitants had hidden their treasures as news of the pirates spread along the California coast. Some families reportedly took their valuables to Mission San Ynez. Santa Barbara was abandoned before Captain Hippolyte arrived. Captain Hippolyte de Bouchard's pirates traded a Spanish prisoner they had captured in Monterey for three pirates who were captured on December 4 at Rancho del Refugio, about twenty-three miles north of Santa Barbara. One Santa Barbara family, headed by Dona Josefa Boronda de Cota, supposedly hid their family silver candlesticks and jewelry in a sixty-foot-deep rock-lined shaft, which could have been a public well. Since the bottom twenty feet of the shaft were full of water, none of the family could recover their treasure after the pirates left. Dona Josefa, James Burke's wife, died in 1882. The shaft or well later collapsed. A parking garage supposedly covers the site now, which was near the county courthouse near Anacope Street.

Skeleton Island Treasure
Skeleton Island was reportedly where pirates cached treasure among Indian graves. Indians killed the pirates and buried them over their loot. Bouchard's treasure was also said to have been hidden on Skeleton Island, but he never found enough treasure to bury.

Solvang Mines and Mexican Caches

Jose de Jesus Pico reported that flasks of quicksilver were secretly used in the area mission to refine ore from mines in the Solvang area. An old Indian supposedly arrived at Mission Santa Ynez with large gold nuggets from a mine whose location he hid. Some tried to follow the Indian back to his mine but lost the trail north of Solvang on a tributary of the Santa Ynez River. Mexican miners in the 1800s supposedly cached their gold near the mouth of Cachuma Creek and never retrieved it.

Vásquez Gaviota Pass Loot

Bandit Vásquez reportedly hid $60,000 in loot in the Gaviota Pass area.

Yankee Blade

The 1,767-ton gold rush U.S. sidewheel steamer *Yankee Blade* was built in 1853 and was 274 feet long with a beam of 34 feet. It hit a pinnacle off Anacapa Island just north of Destroyer Rock on December 3, 1853, after leaving San Francisco in the fog. This site was where U.S. Navy Destroyer Squadron 11 ran onto rocks on September 8, 1923, in fog due to a navigation error. The *Yankee Blade* was said to have been carrying $100,000 to $2 million in gold ($153,000 in gold specie and passenger funds). Anywhere from fifteen to forty people were estimated to have died on the wreck or trying to get to shore. Salvage of gold occurred soon after the wreck. The *Dancing Feather* reported $68,000 in treasure salvaged in November 1854, and the *Pilgrim* reportedly salvaged two chests with $34,000. More than $80,000 was also salvaged by the ship's master Harry Randall. The ship's cannons, ship's bell, a few nuggets and other artifacts have been salvaged also. Today, the wreck is in a difficult area to dive, with limited visibility. The wreck has broken up over time and scattered under fifteen to sixty feet of water. It is in waters adjacent to Vandenberg Air Force Base.

Santa Clara County

Saddlemaker's Treasure

On the Santa Clara (Bernal) Ranch in Santa Clara Valley, a saddle maker supposedly cached $100,000 in gold coins and bars near a stone tanning vat south of San Jose. This could be near Santa Teresa Spring on the Santa Teresa Ranch. He died and took the secret of his fortune's location with him.

SANTA CRUZ COUNTY

PICKETT'S CACHE

In the early 1840s, J.H. Pickett supposedly cached $40,000 on his San Augustino Rancho near Santa Cruz. Mexican General José María Sánchez claimed that Pickett was a revolutionary and threatened him. Pickett joined the California Bear Flag Revolt in 1846 during the Mexican-American War. Pickett died before he could recover his treasure.

Around 1915, a family leased several ranches where Pickett supposedly hid his treasure. This family later left the area and lived a luxurious life in San Francisco, so some believed that they found Pickett's treasure.

SHASTA COUNTY

AVERY BOLE'S LOST MINE

This lost mine was said to have been near Shasta.

JOAQUIN MURIETTA LASSEN PARK TREASURE

Bandit Joaquin Murietta supposedly hid treasure near Shasta in one of the lava caves in Lassen National Park.

Mount Shasta towers over the Central Valley and has a lost gold mine legend. *Author's collection.*

LOST DONKEY MINE
A prospector traveling from the headwaters of Cow Creek to Belle Vista found a rich gold deposit from which he got two sacks of gold. He supposedly made two trips to the mine from Redding before his two mules were found wandering about—the prospector had vanished.

LOST HUMBUG MINE
This is reportedly on the west slope of Humbug Mountain near Redding.

LOST VOLCANO LAKE OF GOLD
See Calaveras County.

LOST WATERFALL MINE
This is supposedly located in Bear Canyon on Bear Creek close to Linwood.

PROSPECTOR'S MIDDLE CREEK NUGGETS
About $25,000 in gold nuggets was claimed to have been buried by a prospector on Middle Creek about five miles upstream of Redding.

RATTLESNAKE DICK CACHE
Outlaw Rattlesnake Dick, whose real name was Dick Barter, reportedly hid treasure in the Trinity Mountains. In the summer of 1856, his gang stole $100,000 in gold being moved from Yreka, Siskiyou County. The robbery occurred just south of Redding in the area of California Highway 273. Another version of this story claimed that it was $106,000 in gold from two stagecoach robberies that were cached. The treasure may have been moved by the gang to the Igo or Cloverdale area and cached. Rattlesnake Dick was captured, went to jail and was killed in July 1859 after he got out of jail. The rest of Rattlesnake Dick's gang were also captured or killed within two weeks of the robbery. It is likely that some of the gang's cached gold was never recovered.

RENEGADE INDIAN GOLD
In the early 1860s, an Indian band supposedly attacked and killed two miners carrying $40,000 worth of gold on Beegum Creek near present Wildwood. A posse captured the renegade Indians, who told them that they hid the gold in a limestone cave in a pool of water on Beegum Creek. The posse hanged the Indians after the Indians refused to take the posse to the cave. The base of Mount Shasta was another potential cache location.

RIFLE BARREL TREASURE
A gold cache is reportedly located in the Trinity Mountains.

RUGGLES BROTHERS LOOT
The Ruggles brothers stole $15,000 ($4,000, $40,000, $50,000 or $75,000) in gold bars from a Wells Fargo stagecoach that left Weaverville bound for Redding on May 14, 1892. The robbery was called the Blue Cut Stage Robbery, near what now is called Ruggles Gulch about six miles from Redding and a mile from Shasta. Near Middle Creek was another location mentioned in a story. Charlie Ruggles had worked in a mine at Iron Mountain north of Shasta and John D. Ruggles had just gotten out of San Quentin Prison. The Ruggles brothers were said to have been from Tulare County, where their family had a ranch. During the robbery, they killed guard Buck Montgomery and wounded the driver and the passenger. Twenty-two-year-old Charles Ruggles was shot in the face with a shotgun blast, and John D. Ruggles thought that he would die so he left Charles behind and took Charles's horse to carry the gold from the strongbox. Another version of the story claimed that they were afoot, but this seems unlikely.

Expecting a posse soon, John supposedly hid most of the loot near Red Bluff, possibly in a cave. Charles was found and captured. One version indicates that John Ruggles dropped a sack of gold in a pig pen near Redding. Authorities searched for John Ruggles for five weeks before his aunt in Woodland notified the law that he was in Woodland, Yolo County. Ruggles was confronted by the lawmen in a Woodland restaurant and captured after he was shot in the neck. In John Ruggles's pocket was $700. The rest of the gold was not found. Both Ruggles brothers were then held in the Redding jail. On July 23, after midnight, some seventy-five citizens broke into the county jail and hanged the outlaws from a cross beam at a nearby blacksmith shop. Wherever the loot was stashed, it was reportedly never found. Some said that it was near Anderson and Cottonwood, but it could have been in several places between Shasta and Woodland.

SIERRA COUNTY

GREENWOOD'S LAKE OF GOLD
Caleb Greenwood claimed that he found a lake with its shores lined with gold nuggets in 1849. A search party went looking for the gold but never

found it. Likely it was at Lake Weber, and Greenwood was paid money to help with the futile search.

Joaquin Murietta Downieville Loot
Joaquin Murietta supposedly hid two caches of $125,000 and $75,000 near Downieville.

Lost Castle Ravine Mine
Miners Johnny Dodge, Bill Haskins and another person supposedly found a rich gold deposit in Castle Ravine near Downieville. They dug out $50,000 in gold and took their treasure to San Francisco, where they boarded ships for New York City. They reportedly never returned, so their rich mine could still remain, but it likely was mined out.

Lost Gibbs Mine
This is reportedly in the Sierra City area.

Lost Lake of Gold
In May 1850, Boston greenhorn Gibbs told J. Goldsborough Bruff that he and his uncle had discovered gold on the shoreline of a lake about five miles long with three towering buttes west of the Pit River. Gibbs claimed that they recovered $5,000 in gold nuggets before hostile Indians drove them off. Gibbs's uncle left for Boston, so Gibbs needed a party to help him mine. Bruff and Peter Lassen formed a prospecting party with Gibbs but found no gold. Sardine Lake just north of Sierra City fit the description but had no gold-lined shore. Lassen was killed by Indians later in Nevada.

Peyton's Lost Treasure
Mexican bandits murdered French shopkeeper Jerome Peyton on November 21, 1861, in the Poker Flat mining district, about ten miles north of Downieville. Peyton reportedly had money cached in nearby hills that has not been recovered.

Stoddard's Lake of Gold
In 1849, Stoddard and a companion became lost and reportedly found a shoreline of a lake covered in nuggets. Indians killed his companion and wounded Stoddard. Stoddard stumbled into a mining camp at Downie's Flat on the North Fork of the Feather River. He later led a large group of prospectors looking for the lake of gold but never found it. After almost

getting lynched by the other prospectors, Stoddard fled. Stoddard always claimed that his story was true. Gold Lake in northern Sierra County gets its name from this search.

SISKIYOU COUNTY

ANDERSON LOST GOLD MINE
The Anderson Lost Gold Mine was rumored to be located in the Mount Shasta area.

CASTLE CRAG'S TREASURE
Near Dunsmuir, $210,000 in gold bars may have been hidden near Castle Crag.

LOST FRENCHMAN MINE
This is said to be located close to Happy Camp on the Indian River.

LOST HAWKINS MINE
Five prospectors traveled from Yreka (Shasta Butte City) and found a rich ledge near the McCloud River. Indians massacred four of the prospectors. Only a man named Hawkins survived, as he was away from the camp tending to their horses when the Indians attacked. Hawkins crossed the McCloud River and made it to settlers' camps. He returned to the area but couldn't find the ledge or their camp. The lost mine may be about seven miles east of McCloud. Hawkins later died in a Shasta hospital.

LOST VOLCANO LAKE OF GOLD
See Calaveras County.

RATTLESNAKE DICK CACHE
See Shasta County.

WEED OUTLAW LOOT
Outlaws supposedly robbed the Lassen–San Francisco stagecoach of $128,000 in gold coins near Weed on May 17, 1859. Wells Fargo had two boxes of $50 gold pieces aboard the stage. The robbers put the coins into their saddlebags. A Shasta City posse arrived on the scene quickly, as it had been after another outlaw in the area. The stagecoach's horses had been run

off. On the west side of Mount Shasta, the posse found two pack animals carrying empty saddlebags, so it was believed that the outlaws cached the gold. Three miles down the road, the posse overtook the robbers and killed them all. Thinking that the gold was buried nearby, the posse spent considerable time searching the area but reportedly found nothing.

SOLANO COUNTY

WILCOX'S FORTUNE

In 1884, wealthy farmer J. William Wilcox reportedly hid more than $50,000 in gold coins on Andrus Island near his home. He came to California in 1852 and established levees around the lowlands in the Sacramento and San Joaquin Delta to farm the rich black soil. He had grape vineyards. He loaned money to his neighbors and friends. His home was about half a mile upriver from Isleton. After Wilcox died, no one knew where he hid his money.

YOSEMITE'S GOLD

The *Yosemite* was a 631- to 1,317-ton steamboat, 283 feet long, built in 1863 at San Francisco, California. On October 22, 1865, after the steamer left the Rio Vista wharf on the Sacramento River with 350 passengers and nearly 1 ton of gold and silver, the *Yosemite*'s starboard boiler blew up. At least 29 Chinese people and 13 to 22 others were killed. Another source claimed that 160 died and 60 were injured. The *Yosemite* and its contents were later raised. The raised *Yosemite* was cut in half, and 36 feet were added to it during reconstruction. It was returned to service.

SONOMA COUNTY

BANDITS CACHE

In 1888, bandits reportedly cached more than $20,000 in gold coins on the summit of County Road 29 just north of the Sonoma County line.

LOST CATTLE BUYERS GOLD

Two cattlemen from Chile supposedly carried $80,000 in gold to Nicholas Higuera's Rancho near Warm Springs in the Lake Sonoma area to purchase cattle. While a fiesta was held in their honor, the two Chileans became ill with cholera and died. The fiesta guests fled. Higuerra ordered his Indian workers to bury the two bodies and their contaminated gold far away from his ranch house.

PAYROLL CACHE
See Napa County.

STANISLAUS COUNTY

LEITH FERRY CACHE
A gold coins cache was reportedly buried close to Leith Ferry not far from Oakdale.

LOST GOLD SAFE
In January 1862, huge winter floods ravaged the Sierra Nevada Mountains and the Sacramento and San Joaquin Valleys. The record flooding swept away many mining camps and towns. One Knight's Ferry area store and its contents disappeared into the floodwaters of the Stanislaus River. Among the lost contents was the store's safe containing gold. No one was ever known to have recovered the safe or the gold.

LOST MEXICAN MINE
The Lost Mexican Mine was said to have been hidden near Sonora Pass.

TEHAMA COUNTY

BIDWELL'S LOST GOLD SHIPMENT
See Butte County.

PETER LASSEN CACHE
Dane Peter Lassen settled in California before it became part of the United States. He was a don who supposedly buried a fortune in gold near Lassen's ranch at the junction of Deer Creek and the Sacramento River. Lassen was murdered along with a companion on April 29, 1859, while in Nevada prospecting for silver.

RUGGLES BROTHERS LOOT
See Shasta County.

Trinity County

Bottles of Gold Dust and a Pouch of Gold Coins
In the Big Flat area, about nine miles west of Helena, ten stone bottles of gold dust and a leather pouch filled with gold coins were supposedly cached.

Fisher Gulch Copper Chests of Gold
Three copper chests full of gold worth more than $100,000 reportedly were buried by Big Jim Fisher along Canyon Creek, which empties into the Trinity River about twenty miles above Weaverville.

Klamath Mountains Gold
Indians were said to have murdered two miners about 1860 and placed almost $40,000 worth of gold in a pit not far from the Hall City Cave in the Klamath Mountains west of Weaverville. The Indians were captured and hanged, so the gold was lost.

Lost Poker Cache
In the fall of 1863, Lieutenant Jonas Wilson led seven soldiers chasing renegade Indians. At Soldier's Grove, below Showers Pass in Humboldt County, a courier arrived with seven months' back pay in gold for the soldiers.

Trinity County settlers reported an Indian uprising, so the patrol left camp to help. For twenty-eight hours straight, they rode southeast through Round Mountain and Kettenpom Peak to what later became Zinia. The patrol reached the upper Hoaglin Valley at sunset, where the men camped at the base of Haman Ridge.

They played poker with their pay, and most lost their money to Lieutenant Wilson, who had a run of good luck. Under an old oak tree that had been hit by lightning, Lieutenant Wilson reportedly hid his pouch filled with gold coins before the patrol rode off. During a fight with Indians, Lieutenant Wilson was killed, and his poker cache was supposedly never found.

I searched Civil War California military records, which had numerous Wilsons listed but no Jonas. Maybe Jonas was a nickname. My search of the *Official Records* didn't have a skirmish listed, but small action reports during the Civil War were often not filed.

Rattlesnake Dick Gang's Trinity Mountain Loot
In 1856, outlaw Rattlesnake Dick Barter's gang reportedly stashed $40,000 of an $80,000 bullion robbery on a Trinity Mountain trail near Cecilville

Gold mining dredges such as this one in Trinity County moved vast quantities of rock and soil to mine buried gold. *New York Public Library*.

near the Humboldt County/Trinity County line. Rattlesnake Dick and Cyrus Skinner were supposed to have stolen pack mules to meet George Skinner, Dolph Newton, a man named Carter and Luis Romero, who actually robbed the mule train. Rattlesnake Dick and Cyrus Skinner did not show up with mules since they had been arrested while trying to steal the mules near Folsom. Unable to carry all the bullion, the robbers buried half the loot and took the other half to meet the rest of the gang near Folsom. Wells Fargo agent Jack Barkeley and a posse captured Dolph Newson, Luis Romero and Carter near the Mountaineer House on the Folsom-Auburn Road. George Skinner was killed while resisting arrest. Newton and Romero were sent to jail for ten years. Carter copped a plea and revealed where $40,000 was hidden near Folsom, which was recovered. The other $40,000 was reportedly just cached by George Skinner, and he was dead. This could be in Humboldt County.

SHERIFF'S LOST GOLD
When the county sheriff was crossing a rain-swollen creek near Weaverville in April 1862, his saddlebag with $1,000 in gold (worth about $17 per ounce then) tumbled off his horse. The high, swift floodwaters carried the saddlebag downstream on the bottom of the creek. A $250 reward for the

gold's recovery was offered by the sheriff. Miners diverted the creek and searched for the saddlebag with gold but never reported finding it.

Tobey Bierce's Cache
Rancher Tobey Bierce sold horses for about eight hundred silver dollars around 1900 and was thought to have buried them at his camp at Bierce Meadow (now Cleveland Meadow) in the South Fork of the Trinity River area. He got ill and died in Redding.

Tulare County

German's Lost Ledge
In Kings Canyon, a German prospector in 1860 was thought to have camped with his dog on the South Fork of the Kings River maybe nine miles north of where it forks. After chasing his dog, he was tired and took a deer trail through brushy areas, having to crawl at times. In one location, he found rich gold ore that looked like pipe-clay. The man took his samples into town to record his claim but was too late to record it. He went drinking at the saloon, told everyone about his rich find and got into a poker game. The next morning, he was found murdered for his gold near the saloon. In 1877, a group searched for the lost ledge but didn't find it. Although it was thought to be only an hour or two hours' walk from his campsite, no one found the lost ledge.

Haunted Lost Mine
This is said to be located on or near Deer Mountain.

Tuolumne County

Big Oak Flat Gold
High-grade ore was reportedly cached near Big Oak Flat. Also, there was a mine with gold in hard blue schist in this area. These were reportedly west of Yosemite in Big Creek Basin.

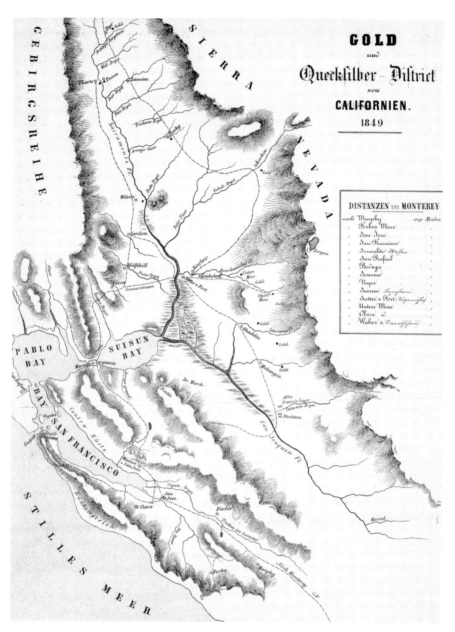

Central California gold mines are mostly in the Mother Lode, with some on the coast. This 1849 map is in German. *Library of Congress.*

Chinese Camp Cache

Two Chinese tongs reportedly fought near Chinese Camp in a pitched battle on September 26, 1856, with more than one thousand people fighting. Four were reportedly killed, including Lee-Yan Chee Wo, who had buried about $50,000 belonging to one of the tongs. The area around his cabin was searched by his tong, but reportedly the cache was never found.

Columbia Gold

A wagon hauling $600,000 in newly minted gold coins from the Columbia Mint in 1854 (or 1850) was reportedly robbed by outlaws. These robbers cached the gold in a cave near Twain Harte. Several days later, all the robbers were killed by a posse in a gunfight. Treasure hunter Frank Fish hunted for this cache and found several 1850 $20 gold coins where he believed this robbery took place.

Frank Fish Found Treasure

Near Columbia, treasure hunter Frank Fish found $870 worth of gold nuggets (1960s value) in an olla and old silver dollars in a small bean pot at the site of a burned-down cabin.

Jackass Hill Cache

A man was murdered at the mining camp of Jackass Hill on the Robinson's Ferry-Tuttletown Trail. He was said to have hidden his fortune nearby.

Joaquin Murietta Tuolumne Loot

Outlaw Joaquin Murietta supposedly hid some of his loot near Tuolumne.

Kettle of Gold

In or near Columbia (or one mile east of Columbia on a ranch), $25,000 in gold and silver coins in a kettle were reportedly buried. The owner was murdered, and his treasure was reportedly not found.

Lost Portuguese Mine

Not far from Columbia, the Lost Portuguese Mine with reportedly $100,000 in gold was hidden by a miner originally from Portugal. He would visit Columbia and exchange mined gold for gold coins. He would then go back to his mine after dark, taking different directions out of town and evading anyone who might follow him. He eventually stopped coming to town, and several weeks later his body was discovered. He had become deathly ill and left a note in Portuguese revealing that he had a rich mine and hidden gold within it. He gave no directions for where the mine was located.

LOST SONORA PASS LEDGE
See Mono County.

LOST TWO POUNDS OF GOLD
A miner supposedly buried two pounds of gold in a pickle jar under a bush before going to Sonora. After returning from celebrating in Sonora, his mind was a bit fuzzy, so he couldn't remember which bush he hid his gold under. The miner and his friends dug under many bushes but never recovered the pickle jars with gold.

OUTLAW WILLIAM MINER CACHE
Outlaw William Miner was in the area of China Camp and may have cached loot there.

THE PORTMAN LOST GOLD MINE
There was a tale that the lost Portman Gold Mine was near the Columbia area.

TOM BELL CAVE LOOT
Outlaw Tom Bell was rumored to have hidden loot in the Moaning Cave or Mercer Caverns north of Sonora. See TOM BELL SAN JOAQUIN LOOT, San Joaquin County.

TOM DAVIS CACHE
At Columbia, Tom Davis reportedly cached $3,000 (or $5,000) in gold ore among three marked pine trees before he left for the Fraser River, British Columbia, Canada gold rush with some fellow miners. After two years, Davis returned to Columbia and discovered that all the trees where he had buried his gold had been cut down and removed. He searched for his gold but never found it.

VENTURA COUNTY

LOST BRAGG MINE/LOST PADRE MINE
In the 1870s, in the mountains north of Piru, Dr. B.F. Bragg reportedly discovered a lost padre mine and obtained a small fortune from it. Dr. Bragg

and one of his neighbors got into a fight. Dr. Bragg hid his mine by causing a landslide over the entrance. Later, a group of men from Neenach (or Neenah) reportedly found the Lost Bragg Mine in 1941 on Sawmill Mountain, but this claim is disputed.

Lost Diamonds Cache

About $100,000 worth of diamonds was supposedly hidden on White Mountain.

Lost Mission Mine/Los Lost Padres Mine/Lost Padre Placer

In the 1860s, a prospector reportedly discovered an abandoned Spanish mine. He claimed that it was about three days' ride from Fort Tejon in a clearing about 1.5 miles from a spring. Before he could lead anyone to the mine, the prospector was killed when his horse threw him from his saddle. Some claimed that they found the spring but not the mine.

Fort Tejon was built in 1854 by the U.S. Army at the head of Grapevine Canyon to guard Tejon Pass, a key crossing over the Coastal Range on the Overland Road from Los Angeles to San Francisco. Fort Tejon was the home of the U.S. Army's camel cavalry for several years before the Civil War. It is now a California State Historic Park adjacent to I-5 just north of Lebec.

Mission San Fernando Rey de Espana (Holy King Ferdinand of Spain) padres traveled throughout this area to minister to Indians and to look for gold and silver. An old Spanish (or Indian) gold or silver mine reportedly was south of Fort Tejon in the Coastal Range Mountains. Smelting furnaces to refine the ore were located in San Emigdio Canyon. The padres at Mission San Luis Obispo de Tolosa reportedly made silver plate from this mine's ore.

Los Padres Mine was reportedly located between Ventura and Fort Tejon, in the San Emigdio Mountains in Los Padres National Forest. Padre Junípero Serra founded Mission San Buenaventura on March 31, 1782, in present Ventura. Indians who attended Mission San Buenaventura showed the mission padres where Los Padres Mine was located. The Indians and padres secretly mined silver and refined the ore in smelters, said to be about a league from the mine.

When Mexico took over the California missions in 1833, the padres supposedly hid the mine's location and dismantled the smelters. It was claimed that the padres put a curse on the mine to prevent Indians from revealing the mine's location. In his later years, an Indian called Carlos Juan may have worked the mine. Some gold mines were later developed in the area called the San Gabriel Gold Mining District.

The mountains and valleys near Fort Tejon have many stories of lost mines and treasure. *Author's collection.*

After Mexican independence, silver bars from Los Padres Mine were supposedly moved to Mission San Luis Obispo de Tolosa for storage. Silver bars were smuggled out of California on American ships that visited the coast, which is also what a Russian visitor to California later wrote.

In 1853, the district attorney of Santa Barbara County, Russell Heath, brought a priest to Carlos Juan to ensure that he was protected from any padre's curse. Carlos Juan still refused to give direction to the cursed mine.

In 1871, when Carlos Juan was over eighty years old, he guided a group to find the mine for a friend, Angel Escandon. Carlos Juan felt obligated to help Angel, as he had aided him earlier in life. Carlos Juan stopped at one area and told the party that the mine was about a league away. He refused to get closer. Padre Juan Comapla tried to convince Carlos Juan that he had absolution and nothing to fear. Carlos Juan showed the party an abandoned smelter site but nothing more.

A recently abandoned mine in the area was found, but it was not Los Padres Mine. The mine tunnel and mining drills and equipment they found were thought to be less than twenty years old.

Some claimed that Los Padres Mine was about forty to fifty miles northwest of Ventura and Santa Barbara, to the west of Fort Tejon. Other stories have it located about forty miles northeast of Mission San Buenaventura. Another possible mine was near Sespe. Many people searched for the lost mine along San Emigdio Creek (or San Emedio Creek) in Santiago Canyon and near Pine Mountain (or Mount Pinos).

MURIETTA RED MOUNTAIN CACHE

Bandit Joaquin Murietta supposedly cached some loot near Red Mountain.

OLIVAS ADOBE TREASURE
Don Ramon Olivas had an adobe house southeast of Ventura on Rancho San Miguel, where he was said to have been robbed of part of his wealth from his vault. After the robbery, Don Olivas allegedly cached his wealth nearby instead of using a vault. After he died, his family looked unsuccessfully for his money.

SAN NICHOLAS ISLAND WRECK
A Spanish galleon supposedly was lost in the 1730s off San Nicholas Island with a cargo of $1 million in treasure.

SANTA SUSANNA PASS CACHES
Bandit Tiburcio Vásquez reportedly hid $60,000 in the Santa Susanna Pass area. Stagecoach robbery loot consisting of buckskins of gold dust was reportedly cached at Spahn's Movie Ranch in the Santa Susanna Pass area. A bandit in 1853 was said to have robbed a stagecoach at Santa Susanna Pass and cached $65,000 in two places, near a spring and a canyon, before dying of wounds.

THREE FINGER JACK LOOT
Near Wheeler Hot Springs, outlaw Three Finger Jack supposedly hid his loot ($20,000) possibly in the Murietta Canyon area, which was named after bandit Juaquin Murietta. Three Finger Jack was killed in 1853.

WINFIELD SCOTT
The 1,291-ton sidewheel steamer *Winfield Scott* was 225 feet long with a 34-foot beam. It was built in 1850 in New York and sank after hitting a rock off Anacapa Island's Frenchy Cove on December 3, 1853, during fog; it did not immediately sink. Its crew and passengers were rowed ashore on Anacapa Island and eventually rescued. It was thought that the ship carried some treasure, but much of it was probably taken off when the passengers went on to the island. The wreck is now scattered about in 20 to 30 feet of water, with most of the metal salvaged in 1894 and during World War II for scrap. Some bottles, dishes and coins have been recovered over the years, but the site is now protected as part of the Channel Islands National Monument.

YOLO COUNTY

RUGGLES BROTHERS LOOT
See Shasta County.

WILLIAM MINER LOOT
Prolific outlaw William Miner was said to have cached $812 in gold near Woodland on the William Miller Ranch.

YUBA COUNTY

BILLY SNYDER'S LOST GOLD
Miner Billy Snyder was a successful placer gold miner on a branch of Oregon Creek on a ridge near Comptonville. Snyder got very sick and supposedly cached his $30,000 worth of gold in a grove of trees by moonlight where the shadow of two tree limbs formed a X. He left his cabin at his claim and went to a doctor in Nevada City, who sent him to a doctor in Sacramento, who then sent him to a doctor in San Francisco. It took him six months to recover. By the time he got back to his claim and cabin, all the trees had been cut down. He was unable to find where he buried his gold.

The Yuba River gold field has mining tailings towering over the Yuba River. *Author's collection.*

Butte Creek Treasure
See Butte County.

California House Loot
A stage station called California House outside Marysville was a base for a band of robbers during the gold rush period. Outlaw Tom Bell reportedly buried $35,000 nearby (possibly Dry Creek Gulch) before he was captured and hanged.

MISSION TREASURES

Due to Russian and English outposts and incursions along the Pacific coast, Spain established missions, presidios and pueblos along the Alta California coast. Padre Junípero Serra founded many of these missions. The first mission was Mission San Diego de Alcalá in 1767. It was followed by twenty Spanish missions along the California coast. El Camino Real (the King's Road) connected all the missions by land. Today, California Highway 1 mostly follows this route.

Each mission had a Spanish military guard usually consisting of four or five soldiers under a sergeant. At each mission, the converted Indians, or neophytes, were mandated to work hard and attend church services, with little time for themselves. The mission Indians were treated as serfs or peons and allowed yearly visits to relatives and friends who lived in distant areas.

When the Spanish began colonizing California, the Indians numbered between 150,000 and 300,000. Only 100,000 Indians are believed to have survived the Mission Period due to raging epidemics and poor treatment. Indians who left the mission system were chased by Spanish soldiers, who forced them to return to the missions. Many tales of lost mines and hidden mission treasures are associated with these missions.

About eight hundred converted and wild Indians attacked Mission San Diego de Alcalá after midnight on November 4, 1775. Padre Luis Jaymes and two other Spaniards were killed by the attacking Indians. The other eight Spaniards in the mission were wounded and fortified themselves in a storeroom. The Indians looted the sacristy and storehouse and burned down most of the mission. The soldiers in the nearby presidio eventually rescued the survivors. From time to time, the California Indians revolted against or fled from the missions. In 1795, almost two hundred Indians left Mission Delores due to the cruelties they suffered.

The first known developed placer deposits were in present Imperial County, California, in 1775 in what became known as the Potholes District, which is about fifty miles east of El Centro and ten miles northwest of Yuma, Arizona, near the Colorado River.

Spain established two pueblos on the Colorado River on the trail between Mission San Diego de Alcalá and Tucson, Arizona. The Spanish pueblos were on the west side of the Colorado River in California at the upper end of navigation on the Colorado River and near the Potholes District. La Purisima Concepcion was a pueblo established in 1780 at what is now Fort Yuma Hill, where the Gila River met the Colorado River. In 1851, the ruined site was described as consisting of eight to ten adobe structures on about one acre of land.

The pueblo of San Pedro y San Pablo de Bicuñer was established in January 1781 in the hills near a Colorado River overflow channel about four or five leagues (eight miles) downstream of La Purisma Concepcion at a Yuma village or rancheria. About 160 Spanish, part-Spanish and civilized American Indians settled in the two towns and missions. Yuma Indians were forced to mine gold in the Potholes, Picacho and Cargo Muchacho-Tumco mining districts in California and in the Laguna Mountains in Arizona.

On July 17, 1781, a simultaneous attack by Yuma (Quechan) Indian warriors and some Mohave Indians took place as Spanish settlers were leaving church services. In La Purisma Concepcion, eleven soldiers were killed. In Bicuñer, seventeen men and Padre Diaz were killed. Bicuñer's church and the town were looted and set afire.

Across the Colorado River on the Arizona side, a detachment of eleven Spanish soldiers made a makeshift barricade that was overrun, with all the Spanish soldiers killed. La Purisma Concepcion was looted and burned on July 18. On July 19, the Indians killed two captured Franciscan padres. Church images were destroyed or thrown away. The Spanish lost four Franciscan padres, thirty-one soldiers, twenty male settlers, twenty women and twenty children, with five soldiers, four settlers and sixty-seven women and children taken captive.

A Spanish expedition led by Lieutenant Colonel Pedro Fages consisting of 110 Spanish soldiers from Tucson and 96 Ootyam Indian allies arrived at the Colorado River in the fall of 1781. They were aided by 600 Indian

Fort Yuma Hill in 1850 from Yuma. Mission La Purisma Conception was destroyed here. There were tales of nearby lost mines and treasure. *Library of Congress.*

allies (Halchichoma, Cocomericopa and Gila River Indians). Just 5 soldiers and 69 survivors from the attacks by the Yumas and Mohaves were safely recovered by trade or rescue. Several battles also took place, with the hostile Indians taking to the hills and hiding. Several stories of lost mines and lost treasures come from these events.

In 1792, Jose Longinos Martinez wrote, "The natives in the vicinity of Mission San Gabriel are accustomed to carry small stones, which they acquire from the Indians who bring them from the Island of Los Angeles (Santa Catalina Island). These stones are of lead in galena with silver." Martinez indicated that the Indians used the stones as magical charms. There is much evidence that silver and gold were found in a number of areas but maybe not reported to Spanish authorities to avoid problems with royalties and permits from the Spanish government.

In 1824, at Mission La Purisma Concepcion, an Indian attack burned down part of the mission with four civilians killed. More than one hundred Mexican soldiers attacked the neophytes at Mission La Purisma Concepcion, and one soldier and sixteen neophytes were killed during the mission's recapture.

At the same time at Mission Santa Barbara, neophytes took over that mission and slashed two guards. Mexican soldiers arrived at Mission Santa Barbara, where four Mexican soldiers were wounded and three Indians were killed. The rebellious neophytes fled eastward into the San Joaquin Valley, with fifty of the neophytes from the Channel Islands going to Santa Cruz Island.

Missionaries were reported to have accumulated "hard cash," which the new Mexican government wanted. The Mexican government decision to confiscate mission wealth and lands was a pretext for its action against the missions. A Russian visitor to California reported that the padres were not keeping their treasure at the missions but rather were converting it to gold for easy transport from the country. Many tales of hidden mission treasures and lost mines came from this period of mission confiscations.

The Spanish Franciscans were replaced with padres with allegiance to the new nation of Mexico. Most of the padres left California for Spain or other

Mission Santa Barbara has legends of nearby lost treasure and mines. *New York Public Library*.

Spanish colonies, like the Philippines. In 1833, the Mexican government confiscated the missions and secularized them.

In 1833, there were about thirty-one thousand Christianized Indians serving twenty-one missions and four presidios staffed by sixty padres and three hundred soldiers. In 1834, the twenty-one Alta California missions had 396,000 cattle, 62,000 horses and 321,000 pigs, as well as sheep and goats, and produced 123,000 bushels of grain. Mexico's California governor Bautista Alvarado gave out or sold twenty-eight land grants between 1836 and 1842 to local Mexican politicians and supporters.

PIRATES AND BOOTY

In 1579, English pirate (privateer to the English) Sir Francis Drake commanded the eighteen-gun, one-hundred-ton *Golden Hind* (formerly *Pelican*) on a pirating expedition consisting of five ships to raid Spanish ships and ports of their treasure while also looking for the fabled Northwest Passage. England at that time was not at war with Spain. The *Golden Hind* was named after Sir Christopher Hutton, a major investor in Drake's expedition. Sir Hutton's coat of arms was a golden hind. Queen Elizabeth I also invested in Drake's expedition. Drake was known as El Draque or "The Dragon" due to his raids in the Caribbean Sea, Central America and South America. Drake's expedition left Plymouth, England, on December 13, 1577, to cross the Atlantic Ocean and then sailed through the Strait of Magellan to the Pacific Ocean. One ship returned to England, one was wrecked and two ships were burned due to being unserviceable.

Off the west coast of South America near Panama, the solitary *Golden Hind* captured the Spanish galleon *Nuestra Senora de la Concepcion* (called *Cacafuego* or *Spitfire*). It took three days to transfer fourteen chests of pieces of eight, eighty pounds of gold, twenty-six tons of silver bars, silver plates, boxes of pearls and jewels to the *Golden Hind*. Each of the *Golden Hind*'s crew reportedly received sixteen bowls of coins. Drake raided the west coast of South America, capturing much treasure from Spanish settlements and ships. Some crewmen were worried about all the weight of gold and silver overloading *Golden Hind* and endangering their trip back to England, so they reportedly threw some treasure overboard and buried some ashore.

The *Golden Hind* carried about thirty-five tons (forty tons) of Spanish treasure when it sailed up the California coast. Not finding the rumored Northwest Passage to the Atlantic Ocean, the *Golden Hind* sailed south down the California Coast. At Drakes Bay, just north of San Francisco Bay, the *Golden Hind* was laid up on a beach and careened to scrape its hull, fill the hull leaks and caulk the ship between June 27 and July 23, 1579. Sir Francis Drake planted the English flag in California, which he called New Albion. Drake dumped several cannons overboard to lighten his ship and supposedly hid treasure. He stopped at the Farallon Islands to stock up on seal meat. Drake circumnavigated the globe, and his rich crew arrived in Plymouth, England, on September 26, 1580. Queen Elizabeth I made Drake a knight in 1581. Drake became a British vice-admiral and led the defeat of the Spanish Armada in 1588. Drake led a number of British naval raids in the Americas and died in 1596. See DRAKE TREASURE, Marin County; DRAKE TREASURE, Monterey County; and *GOLDEN HIND* TREASURE, San Luis Obispo County.

Mexico began to revolt against Spain in 1810 with Padre Hidalgo's "Grito de Dolores." California and other frontier areas often did not receive supplies until after Mexico became independent. In Alta California, the missions, presidios, pueblos and rancherias were self-supporting, as they received little or no assistance from embattled Spain or from Mexican rebels.

In 1818, the pirate (privateer to the rebels) Hippolyte (or Hiplito, Hyppolyte) de Bouchard sailed down the Alta California coast with 260 Argentine, Hawaiian and American pirates in the thirty-eight-gun frigate *Argentina* and twenty-six-gun corvette *Santa Rosa* to capture Spanish ships and raid Spanish settlements. Bouchard had letters of marque from the United Provinces of the Rio de la Plata (Argentina). Bouchard captured and burned the Spanish Alta California capital of Monterey after the *Santa Rosa* was disabled by the Spanish battery El Castillo. Bouchard's privateers cruised down the Alta California coast, raiding and terrorizing Santa Cruz, Rancho de Fufio, Santa Barbara and Mission San Juan Capistrano. Although they searched for treasure, they found none, as the Spanish population fled inland, and the meager Spanish military confronted them whenever the pirates landed. Hippolyte de Bouchard circumnavigated the planet in his hunt for Spanish treasure. See MISSION CARMEL TREASURE, Monterey County; MISSION SAN JUAN CAPISTRANO TREASURE, Orange County; TRABUCO CANYON MINE AND TREASURE, Orange County; SANTA BARBARA TREASURE, Orange County; and SKELETON ISLAND TREASURE, Santa Barbara County.

GOLD AND THE GOLD RUSH

T he Spanish mined placer gold deposits in the Imperial Valley from around 1775 to 1780 in the Potholes District, Picacho District and Cargo Muchacho-Tumco District. The Spanish governor of Alta California, José Joaquín de Arrillaga (1804–14), thought that mining also had possibilities in California and wrote that "the greater part of the mountains gave indications of various minerals" and that "eight or nine marcos of silver" had already been mined from them.

Near Monterey and Santa Cruz, silver ore was mined, but the mines were generally considered unprofitable and later abandoned. In 1828, a small gold placer deposit was discovered at San Ysidro, about twenty-five miles northeast of San Diego.

In 1835, in present Los Angeles County, another small placer gold deposit was known to have been found in San Francisquito Canyon and in 1842 in Placerita Canyon. Mexican Sonorans with mining experience were the primary miners on the Mexican frontier until about 1846.

John Marshall's accidental discovery of gold at Sutter's Mill in Coloma on the American River in what became the Mother Lode Country in 1848 changed California. Hordes of gold seekers swarmed into California from all over the globe. So many people came to California that in 1850 it became the thirty-first American state.

Even Cherokee Indians living in Indian Territory joined the gold rush. Cherokees had been involved in the Georgia and North Carolina Gold Rushes in the 1830s. The community of Cherokee, California, is named after a group of Cherokee gold miners who found gold there. Would-be

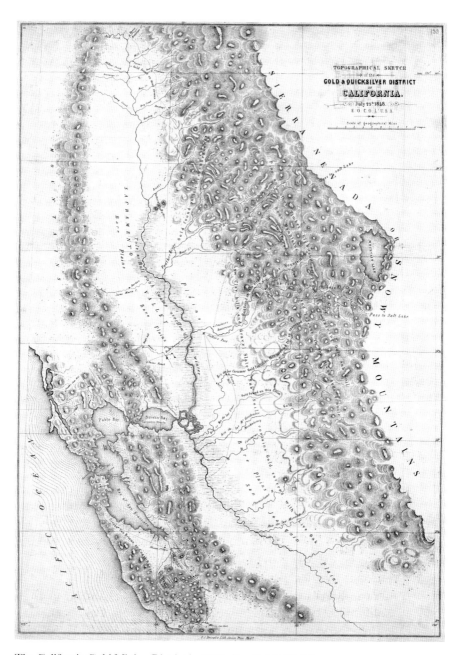

The California Gold Mining District in 1858. *New York Public Library*.

Above: John Marshall stands in front of Sutter's Mill, where he found gold and started the gold rush. *Library of Congress.*

Opposite: An 1848 emigrant's guide encouraging gold seekers to go to California to seek their fortune. *New York Public Library.*

miners sailed from the East Coast around the Cape of Magellan or went by ship to Central America, where they crossed the isthmus and took another ship to California on the Pacific Ocean. Thousands traveled the California Road, Santa Fe Trail and other cross-country routes to California.

Gold deposits are found in many areas of California. The most famous is the Mother Lode region. It was odd that the Spanish and Mexican settlers never reported finding gold in the Mother Lode area of the Sierra Nevada Mountains. Initially, gold nuggets and dust were mined from easy-to-access placer deposits in active rivers and streams by miners using simple tools like picks, shovels and washers. In desert areas, where there was little water, the mining was done using dry washers. Many prospectors were greenhorns unfamiliar with geology and mining.

Most easy-to-mine placer deposits were depleted early by the thousands of miners who swarmed into California. Water was channeled from rivers

THE EMIGRANT'S GUIDE TO THE GOLD MINES.

THREE WEEKS IN THE GOLD MINES,

OR

ADVENTURES WITH THE GOLD DIGGERS OF CALIFORNIA

IN AUGUST, 1848:

TOGETHER WITH

ADVICE TO EMIGRANTS,

WITH FULL INSTRUCTIONS UPON THE BEST METHOD OF GETTING
THERE, LIVING, EXPENSES, ETC. ETC., AND A

Complete Description of the Country.

WITH A MAP AND ILLUSTRATIONS.

BY HENRY I. SIMPSON,

OF THE NEW-YORK VOLUNTEERS.

NEW-YORK:

JOYCE & CO., 40 ANN STREET.

1848.

Price with the Map, Cents.   Price without the Map, 12½ Cents.

Top: A Sierra Nevada mine on top of a mountain, with half the mountain cut away by mining. *Author's collection.*

Bottom: Placer Mine at Volcano, with hydraulic washing of gold-bearing gravels and cobbles. *New York Public Library.*

Opposite: A Yuba gold field dredge that was active in recent years recovering aggregate and gold. *Author's collection.*

and streams to erode away hills and even mountains to reach ancient stream beds with gold. Miners used drifts, tunnels and hard rock mining techniques to recover lode ore. Hydraulic mining of tertiary channel deposits in semi-consolidated rock was also developed, which caused huge problems of flooding and silting up streams, rivers and valleys in the Sacramento River and San Joaquin River basins. Large corporate mining ventures using

dredging, large hydraulic mining projects and large lode mining took place in the Mother Lode region. Other California areas also had extensive subsurface mining. There were hundreds of mines, but there are now only a few active commercial mines today.

When I worked for the U.S. Army Corps of Engineers, I was involved in maintaining the old mining debris structures, especially in the Yuba Gold Field on the Yuba River. These structures were built under the authority of the California Debris Commission to channel mining debris out through the Mother Lode rivers into the San Francisco Bay. Alas, by the time these debris structures were built, gold mining on a large scale had stopped. Most of the mining debris that once clogged rivers has been removed by floods over the years.

During the Great Depression, many people combed California looking for gold and silver, especially in the Mohave Desert. Extensive mining claims exist in most gold regions. Prospectors found various mineral deposits that were not rich enough to mine at that time, but due to product price increases and economic needs, these mineral deposits were often revisited and reviewed for economic viability. During World War II, many mineral deposits not rich in gold were developed due to the need of them for war materials in planes, ships and weapons. During World War II, lode mines were normally shut down, as gold was deemed to not be an essential metal for the war effort.

The miners were needed to mine strategic minerals or serve as soldiers. When World War II ended, most of the gold mines remained closed, as it was too expensive to return them to production at the set gold prices. Many mines had their deep shafts filled with water.

With the dramatic rise in the price of gold since the 1980s, recreational mining used portable dredges and scuba gear to recover placer gold in rivers and streams. Gold nuggets and gold dust continue to move and be deposited downstream of their sources. Mining constraints from the U.S. government and California agencies have restricted or blocked access to many mining areas.

The California gold fields have been mapped and explored over the centuries. The U.S. Geological Survey and State of California published large numbers of reports detailing geology, mining projects and areas with potential for mining. These are very useful for those wishing to mine gold. Learning about the complex regulations will help keep modern gold miners out of trouble.

LOST MINES

L ost mines" can mean a lost once active mine or a mineral deposit that was found and never mined due to its finder being ill, disoriented, murdered, dying from illness and so on. Most California counties have lost mine stories. California probably has more than one hundred lost mine tales. These stories generally were in desert, treasure hunting and mining magazines over the years, with little documentation. I have presented some of the better-known lost mines in this book.

Many lost mine stories came from the early days of the California Gold Rush in the late 1840s to 1870s before major gold mining projects began with hydraulic mining, shaft mining and dredging. These large projects were funded and directed by large mining corporations and syndicates mainly based in San Francisco, New York City and Boston.

The lone prospector with a mule was a solitary individual hunting for a bonanza based on lost mine stories or geological leads on the surface. The lone prospector who finds a large deposit of gold and then can't revisit the bonanza was a popular theme in lost mine tales. Typical lost mine stories in the desert country have the prospector survive Indian attacks or run out of food and water before he stumbles across a rich gold deposit. He often carries samples to civilization before he dies or can't remember where he got the gold samples. Sometimes it appears that all the easy gold was mined, and he left for home or to find other minerals elsewhere.

Lost lakes of gold were a popular theme among gold rush lost mine stories. No real lakes of gold seem to have been mined though. I suspect

Top: A Sierra Nevada rock outcrop with different rock types. *Author's collection.*

Bottom: Early-day gold miner equipped for going to the diggings. *Library of Congress.*

that they saw flakes of mica, which shimmer in sunlight like gold in sand along waterways.

Most lost placer mines were in the Mother Lode region, where there was adequate water supplies from the Sierra Nevada Mountains to provide water for hydraulic mining and dredging. Huge quantities of sand and gravel were mined to get out the small amount of gold trapped there. It is hard to believe that lost placer mines on major rivers and tributaries were not mined by others. Death Valley Scotty was a typical promoter of mines that never existed.

Many lost mines were likely small deposits that were mined out by the finder. Some lode lost mines needed drilling and geological work to determine the extent of the deposit and whether they were economic to mine. Undoubtedly, deeper unmined gold, silver and other mineral lodes exist that have only been surface mined. Tracing surface lode outcrops deeper has led to many economic mineral discoveries.

Hostile American Indians were an issue with many early mines. Undoubtedly, a number of prospectors and miners were killed by Indians and bandits or were run off their claims. Some lost mine tales appear to have been created by prospectors looking for a grub stake so they might actually stumble on a rich gold deposit.

OUTLAWS AND LOOT

The discovery of gold brought in an influx of outlaws who found that it was far easier to rob miners of gold than to actually mine gold. The murder of the Reed family in 1848 (see REED TREASURE AT MISSION SAN MIGUEL ARCANGEL, San Luis Obispo County) started a long history of robberies in California.

Joaquin Murietta may have been as many as five different bandits combined into one narrative during the California Gold Rush. Cherokee writer and publisher John Rollin Ridge (Yellow Bird) wrote his novel *The Life and Adventures of Joaquin Murieta*, published in 1854. Ridge made Joaquin Murietta famous. Some speculate that Murietta and his gang stole more than $150,000 during their robberies. Murietta was said to have been a Sonoran miner who was wronged by the influx of American miners and got his revenge by attacking miners and robbing them. Murietta and his gang may have murdered more than forty miners over several years. Joaquin Murietta was killed by California Ranger Harry Love on July 25, 1853, in Fresno County. Murietta's head was removed so Love had proof. Undoubtedly, other bandits associated with him, including some of his relatives, were involved in robberies. There were even stories that the real Joaquin Murietta was not killed. Stories place loot associated with Joaquin Murietta in Butte, Calaveras, Fresno, Lassen, Los Angeles, Mariposa, Merced, Riverside, San Diego, San Joaquin, Santa Barbara, Shasta, Sierra, Tuolumne and Ventura Counties.

The Tiburcio Vásquez Adobe in Monterey. Vásquez was a noted bandit who reportedly hid much loot in California. *Author's collection.*

Tom Bell was another noted bandit during the gold rush era. His real name was Thomas J. Hodges, and he was from Tennessee. He had been a soldier in the Mexican-American War, claimed to have been a doctor and was an unsuccessful gold miner. Tom Bell was the name he used when he was first captured and sent to prison. Bell escaped the Angel Island prison and committed a number of robberies. He was part of a gang of robbers that terrorized California. Bell was captured at Firebaugh's Ferry by a posse and hanged on October 4, 1856. There was also another robber at the same time called Tom Bell. Tom Bell treasures were reportedly in Amador, Placer, Sacramento, San Joaquin, Tuolumne and Yuba Counties.

Tiburcio Vásquez was a Californio bandit born in Monterey on April 11, 1835. He and his gang terrorized California. He claimed that he was resisting American aggression and wanted California returned to Mexico.

During a robbery of Andrew Snyder's general store at Tres Pinos, a sheepherder was murdered and a number of men shot or injured by Vásquez's gang while they looted the store of provisions and money on August 26, 1873.

A posse from Los Angeles captured Vásquez northwest of Rancho La Berea on May 14, 1874, while Vásquez was trying to fence stolen booty. After a trial for the Tres Pinos robbery Vásquez was hanged on March 19,

1875, in San Diego and buried at the Mission Santa Clara Cemetery. His loot was reportedly cached in Fresno, Kern, Los Angeles, Monterey, San Benito, San Diego, Santa Barbara and Ventura Counties.

Rattlesnake Dick Barter lived in Shasta for a while, as well as at the Mountaineer House on the Folsom-Auburn Road. His gang robbed a bullion-carrying mule train near Shasta. See RATTLESNAKE DICK CACHE, Shasta County, and RATTLESNAKE DICK GANG'S TRINITY MOUNTAIN LOOT, Trinity County.

Charles E. Boles was also called Charles Bolton but is remembered by his outlaw name of Black Bart. He robbed twenty-eight stagecoaches by himself over eight years and left several poems to irritate Wells Fargo agents, including one signed "Black Bart, the PO-8." There appear to be no stories of Black Bart hiding any of his loot.

Between 1870 and 1884, Wells Fargo recorded 340 stagecoach robberies, 4 train robberies and 370 burglaries against the company, with a loss of $415,312.55. From the influx of miners from all over the world during the gold rush, there were likely hundreds of robberies with much loot hidden and never recovered.

SHIPWRECKS

Over the centuries, about one thousand Spanish vessels traveled the Manila galleon route through the Pacific. The Manila galleon *San Augustin* was the first European shipwreck on the California coast. The *San Augustin* explored along the Northern California coast. After anchoring in Drakes Bay, with most of its crew ashore or in its small boat, the *San Augustin* was driven aground and sank in 1595. The crew made it back to New Spain in a small boat after many hardships.

A number of documented and rumored Spanish ships were lost in the Channel Islands along the California coast. Spanish supply ships from New Spain bringing supplies to the scattered California missions and settlements also sank along the California coastline over the years.

Since San Francisco Bay was the shipping point for the Mother Lode and most of Central and Northern California, a number of ships carried treasure as cargo or had passengers with gold and silver. Fog, islands, reefs and storms claimed a number of these vessels.

Much commerce took place along the Pacific Coast, as interior roads were often rocky or difficult to travel. Unpredictable Pacific storms often battered ships and forced them onto the rocky coast.

A few ships were lost in the Sacramento and San Joaquin river systems due to boiler explosions and snagging. A number of vessels were abandoned over the years, including a number in what was called the Big Break in Contra Costa County from a big levee break during a flood.

San Francisco Bay's Golden Gate before the bridge was built. Many ships were lost coming into and out of this area. *Library of Congress.*

Gold rush vessels such as the *Ada Hancock, Belle, Brother Jonathan, Santa Cecilia, Tennessee, Washoe, Winfield Scott, Yankee Blade* and *Yosemite* all sank with treasure on board. From 1849 through 1861, twenty-four ships sank near or in San Francisco Bay. My research for *Encyclopedia of Civil War Shipwrecks* documented ninety-eight California shipwrecks from 1861 to 1865 due to a number of causes.

Most shipwrecks did not contain gold. For the purposes of this book, I have not done extensive shipwreck research. The California State Lands Commission claims any wreck over fifty years old and has a database of more than 1,500 shipwrecks on its website.

BIBLIOGRAPHY

Government Documents

Abandoned Shipwreck Act. "Final Guidelines, Notice." *Federal Register* 55, no. 233 (December 4, 1990): 50,115–45.

California State Lands Commission. *A Map and Record Investigation of Historical Sites and Shipwrecks Along the Sacramento River Between Sacramento City and Sherman Island.* Sacramento, CA: State Lands Commission, 1988.

Clark, William B. *Gold Districts of California.* Bulletin 193, California Division of Mines and Geology. Sacramento, 1980.

Deep Sea Research, Inc. v. The Brother Jonathan, Her Appurtenances, Furniture, Cargo, etc., Defendant, and the State of California, State Lands Commission, Defendants-Intervenors-Appellants, United States of America, Defendant-Intervenor. No. 95-15693. U.S. Court of Appeals for the Ninth Circuit.

Gold-Bearing Gravel of the Ancestral Yuba River, Sierra Nevada, California. U.S. Geological Survey Professional Paper 772, 1974.

Gold Dredging in California. The California State Mining Bureau, Bulletin 36. Sacramento, 1905.

The War of the Rebellion: A Compilation of the Official Records of the Union and Confederate Armies. 128 vols. Washington, D.C.: Government Printing Office, 1880–1901.

Weinman, Lois J., and E. Gary Stickel. *Los Angeles Beach Harbor Areas.* Cultural Resources Survey, prepared for U.S. Army Engineer District, Los Angeles, California, April 1978.

Yoseloff, Thomas, ed. *The Official Atlas of the Civil War.* New York: Harper & Row, 1967.

Newspapers

Daily Dramatic Chronicle (San Francisco, CA). 1865.
Daily Examiner (San Francisco, CA). 1865.
Sacramento (CA) Bee. 1989, 1999.
Sacramento (CA) Union. 1865.

Books

Bancroft, Hubert Howe. *The Works of Hubert Howe Bancroft.* Vol. 2, *History of California, 1801–1824.* San Francisco, CA: History Company Publishers, 1886.

Bauer, Helen. *Californian Gold Days.* Garden City, NY: Doubleday & Company Inc., 1954.

Brausch, Barbara, and Elizabeth Hogan. *Gold Rush Country.* Menlo Park, CA: Lane Books, 1972.

Calabro, Marian. *The Perilous Journey of the Donner Party.* New York: Clarion Books, 1999.

Chartkoff, Joseph L., and Kerry Kona Chartkoff. *The Archaeology of California.* Redwood City, CA: Stanford University Press, 1984.

Childress, David Hatcher. *Lost Cities & Ancient Mysteries of the Southwest.* Kempton, IL: Adventures Unlimited Press, 2009.

Clark, Howard D. *Lost Mines of the Old West.* Buena Park, CA: Ghost Town Press, 1951.

Conrotto, Eugene L. *Lost Gold and Silver Mines of the Southwest.* Mineola, NY: Dover Publications, 1991.

Corle, Edwin. *The Royal Highway, El Camino Real.* Indianapolis, IN: Bobbs-Merrill Company Inc., Publishers, 1949.

Day, A. Gore. *Pirates of the Pacific.* New York: Meredith Press, 1968.

Dmytryshun, Basil, E.A.P. Crowhart-Vaughan and Thomas Vaughan, ed. and trans. *The Russian American Colonies: Three Centuries of Russian Eastward Expansion, 1798–1867.* Vol. 3. Portland, OR: Oregon Historical Society, 1989.

Dobie, J. Frank. *Coronado's Children: Tales of Lost Mines and Buried Treasures of the Southwest.* New York: Literary Guild of America, 1931.

Douglass, Darren. *Guide to Shipwreck Diving: Southern California.* Houston, TX: Pisces Books, 1990.

Drago, Henry Sinclair. *Lost Bonanzas.* New York: Pocket Books, 1967.

Englehardt, Zephyrin. *The Missions and Missionaries of California.* San Francisco, CA: James H. Barry Company, 1912.

Forbes, Jack D. *Warriors of the Colorado: The Yumas of the Quechan Nation and Their Neighbors.* Norman: University of Oklahoma Press, 1965.

Foreman, Grant. *Marcy and the Gold Seekers.* Norman: University of Oklahoma Press, 1968.

Gaines, W. Craig. *Civil War Gold and Other Lost Treasure.* Rev. ed. N.p.: Amazon, 2019.

———. *Civil War Gold and Other Lost Treasures.* Conshohocken, PA: Combined Publishing, 1999.

———. *Encyclopedia of Civil War Shipwrecks.* Baton Rouge, LA: Louisiana State University Press, 2008.

———. *Hispanic Treasures of the Western United States.* N.p.: Amazon, 2017.

Gibbs, James A. *Shipwrecks of the Pacific Coast.* Portland, OR: Binford and Mort Publishing, 1971.

Hallenbeck, Cleve. *Land of the Conquistadores.* Caldwell, ID: Caxton Printers, Ltd., 1950.

Hanna, Warren L. *Lost Harbor, The Controversy Over Drake's California Anchorage.* Berkeley: University of California Press, 1979.

Hardigree, Peggy. *Strike It Rich!: Treasure Hunting with Metal Detectors.* New York: Harmony Books, 1980.

Hart, Herbert M. *Old Forts of the Far West.* New York: Bonanza Books, 1965.

Hawkins, Bruce R., and David B. Madsen. *Excavation of the Donner-Reed Wagons: Historic Archaeology Along the Hastings Cutoff.* Salt Lake City: University of Utah Press, 1990.

Heizer, Robert F., and Albert B. Elsasser. *The Natural World of the California Indians.* Berkeley: University of California Press, 1980.

Henson, Michael Paul. *America's Lost Treasures.* South Bend, IN: Jayco Publishing Company, 1984.

Holden, William M. *Sacramento: Excursions into Its History and Natural World.* Fair Oaks, CA: Two Rivers Publishing Company, 1987.

Horner, Dave. *The Treasure Galleons: Clues to Millions in Sunken Gold and Silver.* New York: Dodd, Mead & Company, 1971.

Houghton, Eliza P. Donner. *The Expedition of the Donner Party and Its Tragic Fate.* Audiobook.

The Indians of California. Alexandria, VA: Time Life Books, 1994.

Iversen, Eva C. *California's Mission San Miguel Arcangel.* Old Mission San Miguel, CA: Franciscan Padres, n.d.

King, Joseph A. *Winter of Entrapment: A New Look at the Donner Party.* Rev. ed. Walnut Creek, CA: K&K Books, 1994.

Krell, Dorothy, and Paul C. Johnston, eds. *The California Missions.* Menlo Park, CA: Sunset Books, 1999.

Lonsdale, Adrian, and H.R. Kaplan. *A Guide to Sunken Ships in American Waters.* Arlington, VA: Compass Publications Inc., 1964.

Lytle, William M., and Forrest R. Holdcamper. *Merchant Steam Vessels of the United States: 1790-1868—"The Lytle Holdcamper List."* Edited by C. Bradford Mitchell. Staten Island, NY: Steamship Historical Society of America Inc., 1975.

Marinacci, Mike. *Mysterious California, Strange Places and Eerie Phenomena in the Golden State.* Los Angeles, CA: Panpipes Press, 1988.

Marshall, Don B. *California Shipwrecks.* Seattle, WA: Superior Publishing Company, 1978.

———. *Oregon Shipwrecks.* Portland, OR: Binfords & Mort Publishing, 1984.

Marx, Robert F. *Buried Treasure of the United States: How and Where to Locate Hidden Wealth.* New York: Bonanza Books, 1980.

———. *Shipwrecks of the Americas.* New York: Dover Publications Inc., 1987.

Marx, Robert F., and Jennifer Marx. *The Search for Sunken Treasure: Exploring the World's Lost Shipwrecks.* Toronto, CAN: Key Porter Books, 1996.

McDonald, Douglas. *Nevada Lost Mines and Buried Treasures.* Las Vegas: Nevada Publications, 1981.

McGlashan, Charles Fayette. *History of the Donner Party.* San Francisco, CA: A. Carlise & Company, 1922.

Mitchell, John D. *Lost Mines & Buried Treasure Along the Old Frontier.* Glorietta, NM: Rio Grande Press Inc., 1970.

Nesmith, Robert I., and John S. Potter Jr. *Treasure…How and Where to Find It.* New York: ARCO Publ. Company, 1968.

Parker, Carlyle J. *A Personal Name Index to Orton's Records of California Men in the War of the Rebellion, 1861–1867.* Detroit, MI: Gale Research Company, 1978.

Patterson, Richard. *Historical Atlas of the Outlaw West.* Boulder, CO: Johnson Books, 1993.

Penfield, Thomas. *Buried Treasure in the U.S. and Where to Find It.* New York: Grosset & Dunlap, 1969.

———. *Dig Here!* San Antonio, TX: Naylor Company, 1971.

———. *A Guide to Lost Treasure in California.* Deming, NM: Carson Enterprises, 1982.

Pickford, Nigel. *The Atlas of Ship Wrecks & Treasure: The History, Location, and Treasures of Ships Lost at Sea.* New York: Dorling Kindersley Publishing Inc., 1994.

Pierce, R.A. *Lost Mines and Buried Treasure of California: Fact, Folklore, and Fantasy Concerning 110 Sites of Hidden Wealth.* Berkeley, CA: self-published, 1962.

Potter, John S. *The Treasure Diver's Guide.* Garden City, NY: Doubleday & Company, 1960.

Powers, Dennis M. *Treasure Ship: The Legend and Legacy of the S.S. Brother Jonathan.* 2nd ed. N.p.: Maritime Series of Sea Ventures Press, 2006, 2014.

Reinstedt, Randall A. *Ghosts, Bandits & Legends of Old Monterey Carmel and Surrounding Areas.* Carmel, CA: Ghost Town Publications, 1974.

———. *Monterey's Mother Lode: A Pictorial History of Gold in the Santa Lucias.* Carmel, CA: Ghost Town Publications, 1979.

———. *Tales and Treasures of California's Missions.* Carmel, CA: Ghost Town Publications, 1992.

———. *Tales, Treasures and Pirates.* Carmel, CA: Ghost Town Publications, 1976.

Richman, Irving Berdine. *California under Spain and Mexico, 1535–1847.* New York: Cooper Square Publishers Inc., 1965.

Schurmacher, Emile C. *Lost Treasures and How to Find Them.* New York: Paperback Library, 1968.

Steiger, Brad. *Treasure Hunting.* New York: Ace Books Inc., 1967.

Stewart, George R. *Ordeal by Hunger: The Story of the Donner Party.* New York: Ace Books, 1968.

Temple, Sydney. *The Carmel Mission: From Founding to Rebuilding.* Fresno, CA: Valley Publishers, 1980.

Terry, B.V. *Roadmap to Lost Mines and Buried Treasures of California.* Van Nuys, CA: Varna Enterprises, 1980.

Terry, Thomas P. *Treasure Map Atlas.* Wisconsin: Specialty Products, 1974.

Uhrowczik, Peter. *The Burning of Monterey.* Los Gatos, CA: Cyril Books, 2001.

Williamson, Brad, and Choral Pepper. *Lost Treasures of the West.* New York: Holt, Reinhart & Winston, 1975.

Wiltse, Ernest A. *Gold Rush Steamers of the Pacific.* Lawrence, MA: Quarterman Publications Inc., 1976.

Young, Otis E., Jr. *Western Mining: An Informal Account of Precious-Metals Prospecting, Place, Lode Mining, and Milling on the American Frontier from Spanish Times to 1873.* Norman: University of Oklahoma Press, 1970.

Articles

Aldridge, Jim. "The Lost Schwartz Diggings." *True Treasure* 7, no. 8 (July–August 1973): 40.

———. "Treasures of the Mission Santa Ysabel." *Treasure World* 7, no. 7 (June–July 1973): 31–32, 61.

Bishop, Edward Allen. "Lost Sierra Gold." *True Treasure* 5, no. 2 (January–February 1971): 15.

Black, Jack. "Lost Padres Mines." *Western Treasures* 3, no. 5 (June 1968): 24–25, 62–65.

Broadman, James E. "Lost Cement Mine." *Treasure World* 9, no. 1 (December–January 1975): 40–42.

Brouwer, Jake. "The Mysterious Sinking of the Ada Hancock." *Lost Treasure* 21, no. 8 (August 1996): 50–51.

Brown, Steve. "Butte Creek Cache." *Lost Treasure* 1, no. 2 (January 1976): 59–60.

Chandler, George. "Last Cruise of the YANKEE BLADE." *True West* 24, no. 2 (November–December 1976): 24–25, 54–55.

Clark, William B. "Diving for Gold in California." *Treasure Diver* 2, no. 1 (April 1990): 8–10, 12–13, 430–41, 65.

Concoles, Trini. "Lost Treasure of the Galleon, San Francisco Xavier." *Lost Treasure* 22, no. 6 (June 1977): 9–10.

Coutare, J.A. "Ghost Town Treasure." *Treasure World* 7 no. 9 (August–September 1973): 32–22, 36–37.

Dillon, Charles W. "Outlaw Cache on Middle Creek." *True Treasure* 2, no. 6 (September–October 1968): 23–26.

Eberich, Gerry. "The Donner Tragedy—and Treasure." *True Treasure* 7, no. 6 (May–June 1973): 42–44, 49–58.

———. "The $50,000 Andrus Island Treasure Hoard." *True Treasure* 6, no. 12 (December 1972): 34–36, 41.

Ferguson, Jeff. "California Treasure Galleon." *True Treasure* 8, no. 4 (March–April 1974): 15.

———. "Pearl Galleon of the California Desert." *Treasure Search* 1, no. 1 (Summer 1973): 52–55, 59.

———. "Tong War Treasure." *Treasure World* 8, no. 5 (April–May 1974): 65–66.

Gaines, W. Craig. "Breyfogle's Lost Gold." *Lost Treasure* 28, no. 3, (March 2004): 8–10.

———. "California's Treasure Island." *Lost Treasure* 30, no. 11 (November 2005): 32–33.

———. "Capistrano Treasure." *Lost Treasure* 29, no. 9 (September 2004): 37–38.

———. "The Don's Stashes." *Lost Treasure* 25, no. 12 (December 2000): 22–23.

———. "Head Off at the Pass: The Donner Party Tragedy." *Treasure Cache 1999 Annual*, 62–66.

———. "The Mine with Many Names." *Lost Treasure* 26, no. 12, (December 2001): 30–31.

———. "San Diego Treasures." *Lost Treasure* 27, no. 8 (August 2002): 43–45.

———. "San Miguel Arcangel's Treasures." *Lost Treasure* 31 no. 8 (August 2006): 42–43.

———. "Silver and Gold Mines." *Lost Treasure* 24, no. 11 (November 1999): 28–29.

———. "Snowshoe Thompson's Sierra Gold." *Treasure Cache 2007 Annual*, 12–14.

———. "Water Treasure Along the Shores of Honey Lake." *Lost Treasure* 27, no. 6, (June 2003): 42.

———. "The Yuma's Mines." *Lost Treasure* 2, no. 7 (July 2007): 18.

Garrahy, Stephen T., and David J. Weber. "Francisco de Ulloa, Joseph James Markey, and the Discovery of Upper California." *California Historical Quarterly* 50, no. 1 (March 1971): 73–77.

George, Vivienne L. "Lost Poker Cache." *True Treasure* 4, no. 1 (February 1970): 27.

Hall, Richard. "Lost Frenchman Mine." *Treasure World* 8, no. 1 (December–January 1974): 30.

Hammond, Van. "Log of the Lost Cement Mine." *Lost Treasure* 1, no. 12 (November 1976): 32, 36–38.

———. "The Lost Van Duzen Mine." *Treasure World* 6, no. 5 (April–May 1972): 29.

Hammond, Vern. "Missing Gold at Charlie's Butte." *Lost Treasure* 2, no. 8 (July 1977): 20.

Hardesty, Donald L. "The Archaeology of the Donner Party Tragedy." *Nevada Historical Society Quarterly* 30, no. 4 (Winter 1987): 246–68.

Harrison, Allen. "Kokoweef Update." *Treasure* 22, no. 5 (May 1991): 76–77.

Henson, Michael Paul. "California Ranks No. 1 in Potential Treasure Sites." *Lost Treasure* 8, no. 10 (October 1983): 42–47.

———. "California's Colorful Caches." *Lost Treasure* 14, no. 5 (May 1989): 42–47.

———. "Wells Fargo: A Legacy of Lost Loot." *Lost Treasure* 10, no. 10, (October 1985): 44–48.

———. "Wherever You Look, There's Treasure in California." *Lost Treasure* 11, no. 9 (September 1986): 36–42.

Hollister, Fred. "No Treasure Left on the Yankee Blade." *Treasure* 5, no. 12 (December 1974): 26–31, 48.

Hughes, Pat. "Mohave Desert Gold!" *Lost Treasure* 42, no. 6 (June 2017): 6–8.

Ibanez, Jaime. "Three Dirty Men, Gordier's Golden Cache." *Treasure Cache 1999 Annual*, 84–86.

Jenkins, William. "Clue to the Lost Frenchman Mine." *Treasure World* 6, no. 5 (April–May 1972): 43–44.

Kannenberg, Bud, and Evelinn Kannenberg. "Missing Cache of Silver Coins." *True Treasure* 5, no. 8 (July–August 1971): 27.

Katz, Bob. "49'er Treasure Chest Found in Death Valley Is Bogus." DesertUSA. desertusa.com.

Kildare, Maurice. "Missing Golden Slugs Worth $10,000 Apiece!" *True Treasure* 3, no. 6 (November–December 1969): 15–20.

Klette, William. "The Perfect Recipe: The Lost Cement Mine." *Treasure Cache 2002 Annual*, 39–41.

Knight, Joe R. "Debunking the Lost Dutch Oven Mine." *Gold!*, no. 9 (Winter 1974): 38–40, 72.

Lamance, Thomas. "Tax Collector's Cache of Missing Gold Coins." *Treasure World* 5, no. 1 (December–January 1971): 27–28.

MacDonald, Douglas. "Snowshoe Thompson's Lost Lode." *Lost Treasure* 1, no. 5 (April 1976): 30–31.

Masters, Al. "Amazing Treasure Ship of the California Desert." *True Treasure* 3, no. 1 (January–February 1969): 9–16.

———. "California's Fabulous Dune-Locked Pearl Galleon." *Saga's Treasure Special* 1, no. 1 (1975): 32–35, 74–76.

———. "Lassen's Lost Gold Mine." *Treasure World* 7, no. 7 (June–July 1973): 62–64.

———. "Mojave Desert's Lost River of Gold." *True Treasure* 4, no. 8 (July–August 1970): 16–24.

McCoy, James. "Alvord's Gold, Mojave Desert Gold Deposit Legend Continues." *Treasure Cache 2008 Annual*, 42–44.

Miller, Robert H. "Lost Gold of Bicuner." *Treasure World* 6, no. 5 (April–May 1972): 15–16, 18.

———. "San Augustin Treasure." *Treasure World* 5, no. 9 (September 1971): 24.

Miller, Roger. "Lost Mission Bell Treasure." *Treasure World* 8, no. 9 (August–September 1974): 30.

Miller, Walter H. "The Lost Dutch Oven Mine." *Gold!* 1 no. 1 (1969): 6–7, 46–47.

Mulkey, James E. "Hey, Culligan Man! Kokoweef Mountain's River of Gold." *Treasure Cache 1999 Annual*, 21–24.

Murray, Tom G. "The Lost Lee Mine." *True Treasure* 2, no. 12 (November 1977): 27–28.

Nielsen, Eugene. "California Lost Treasure Galleons." *Treasure Diver* 2, no. 2 (June 1990): 8–9, 46–47, 64.

Ohles, Wally. "The Murders in the Old Mission." Mission San Miguel. missionsanmiguel.org.

Oldham, Chick. "Lost Cement Mine." *Gold!* 1, no. 1 (1969): 21.

Parsons, William. "Trinidad: Oceanside's Treasure Ship—Fact or Fiction." *Groundbreaker* (Third Quarter 2011): 2.

Peterson, T.W. "Treasure of the Brother Jonathan." *Treasure World* 3, no. 4 (October–November 1969): 24–27.

Pierson, Larry J. "The Manila Galleon." *Argosy Treasure Hunting '77 Annual*, 49–51.

Ray, Richard. "Invitation to Treasure Hunters, Help Find Drake's Treasures." *Treasure Search* 12, no. 1 (February 1984): 42–45, 63.

Reinstedt, Randall A. "Lost Padre Mine of the Santa Lucias." *Treasure World* 8, no. 7 (June–July 1974): 26–28, 32–34.

———. "Monterey Peninsula's Hidden Wealth." *Old West* 7, no. 1 (Fall 1970): 38–44, 60–62.

Rhoades, Gale R. "Lost Gold of San Felipe Creek." *Treasure World* 4, no. 7 (June–July 1970): 17–19.

Richards, Chuck. "The Elusive Los Padres Silver." *Treasure World* 7, no. 11 (October–November 1973): 32–36, 38.

———. "Lost Gold Cache of the Ruggles Brothers." *Lost Treasure* 1, no. 7 (June 1976): 42–46.

Riley, Joan. "Brother Jonathan Search Continues." *Treasure Diver* 1 no. 1 (September 1989): 8–12.

Roberts, Jason. "Hoard in Hollywood: The Illusive Juarista Treasure." *Lost Treasure* 27, no. 4 (April 2003): 10–11.

Robertson, Dorothy. "Tapestry Gold of the Panamints." *True Treasure* 4, no. 8 (July–August 1970): 59–62.

Robinson, W.R. "Have We Found the Lost Arch Mine?" *Lost Treasure* 1, no. 8 (July 1976): 59–62.

———. "Where Is the Marsh Gold?" *Treasure World* 8, no. 5 (April–May 1974): 16–20.

Rosenhouse, Leo. "Peter Lassen's Lost Gold." *True Treasure* 6, no. 2 (January–February 1972): 36–38, 43.

———. "Trailing the Tom Bell Treasure." *Treasure World* 7, no. 3 (February–March 1973): 28–31, 33.

———. "Treasure Discoveries on California's Channel Islands." *Western Treasure's Sunken Treasure Annual* (Summer 1973): 6–17.

———. "You Can Search for Wrecked Ships at Golden Gate Bridge." *Lost Treasure* 9, no. 8 (August 1984): 60–63.

Ross, Leonard. "Peter Lassen's Lost Gold." *Treasure, True West Special Edition*, no. 12 (Spring 1975): 14–17, 55–57.

Sanford, James, Jr. "Missing Gold Shipment." *Treasure World* 9, no. 9 (August–September 1975): 60.

Sherrell, Jean. "The Sweet, Sad Song of Yellow Bird, California's Confederate Cherokee." *The Californians* 8, no. 4 (November–December 1990): 17–26.

Sifuentes, Edward. "In Oceanside, Legend of Spanish Treasure Hits Home." *San Diego Union*, August 9, 2013.

Smith, Jeff. "Dr. Markey Hoodwinked the Historical Society." *San Diego Reader*, July 11, 2002.

Smith, William B. "Lost Frenchman Gold." *Treasure World* 8, no.7 (June–July 1974): 15.

Stringfellow, Kim. "Kokoweef: Still Searching for the Lost River of Gold." Mohave Project, August 2016. mohaveproject.org.

Strum, Craig. "The Mission Padres Elusive Hoard." *Treasure Cache 2006 Annual*, 20–25.

Taylor, Richard. "Vallecito's Lost Bandit Loot." *Treasure World* 9, no. 11 (October–November 1975): 13.

Toole, Delos. "Was It Galler or Was It Goler?" *Lost Treasure* 10, no. 7 (July 1986): 47–50.

Townley, John M. "Breyfogle or Pegleg?" *Treasure World* 4, no. 9 (August–September 1970): 20–24.

———. "Breyfogle's Paiute Gold." *True Treasure* 5, no. 10 (September–October 1971): 61–64.

———. "Lost Gold of the Mojave." *True Treasure* 9, no. 4 (March–April 1975): 63–65.

Traywick, Ben T. "Frank Fish's Last Treasure Hunt." *Tombstone News*, March 13, 2009.

———. "The Islands of San Francisco Bay." *Lost Treasure* 11, no. 1 (January 1986): 29–30.

———. "Jim Savage's Lost Barrel of Gold." *Western Treasures* 5, no. 3 (June 1970): 40–41.

———. "Lost Gold from the Mt. Ophir Mint." *Treasure World* 6, no. 11 (October–November 1972): 47–49.

———. "Missing Mason Jar of Gold Coins." *True Treasure* 3, no. 6 (November–December 1969): 26–27.

———. "Missing—40 Tons of Gold and Jewels!" *Lost Treasure* 1, no. 8 (July 1976): 63–64.

———. "Peruvian Treasure of San Francisco Bay." *Western Treasures* 5, no. 4 (August 1970): 38–39.

———. "Yankee Jim's Lost Gold." *Treasure World* 5, no. 5 (April–May 1971): 17–18.

Treasure Diver 3, no. 1. "Shipwrecks of Catalina Island." (January 1993): 34–37.

Vance, Tom. "Golden State Treasures." *Lost Treasure* 28, no. 4 (April 2003): 59–61.

Vesilind, Priit J., and Jonathan Blair (photos). "Lost Gold Bounty from a Civil War Ship." *National Geographic Magazine* 206, no. 3 (September 2004): 108–27.

Wieland, Mary. "Pirates Cove." *True West* 15, no. 2 (November–December 1967): 6–9 and 48.

Internet Sites

California State Lands Commission. www.slc.ca.gov.

California State Lands Shipwreck. "Brother Jonathan." www.slc.ca.gov/shipwrecks.

Enfia. "Snowshoe Thompson: His Life and Adventures." Carson Valley Historical Society, 1991. Enfia.info/snowshoe.htm.

National Park Service. "Continuing the Search for First Known Shipwreck Off Western California Coast." September 16, 1998. www.nps.gov/pore/learn/news/news.

Tahoe Country. www.tahoecountry.com.

Wikipedia.com.

ABOUT THE AUTHOR

Author as a five-year old cowboy.
Author's collection.

W. Craig Gaines is the author of *Civil War Gold and Other Lost Treasure, Revised Edition*; *Hispanic Treasures of the Eastern United States*; *Hispanic Treasures of the Western United States*; *The Confederate Cherokees: John Drew's Regiment of Mounted Rifles*; *Encyclopedia of Civil War Shipwrecks*; *Civil War Gold and Other Lost Treasures*; *Success in Life: 401 Encouraging Thoughts*; *Nostradamus' Curse*; *Great Lost Treasure Never Found*; and other books and articles. The History Press published *Lost Oklahoma Treasure* in 2021 and *Lost Texas Treasure* in 2022. Craig has been interested in lost treasure since seeing the film *Treasure Island* when he was very young. He has written lost treasure stories for a variety of treasure hunting magazines over the years. Craig is an engineer, geologist and writer who has been in many of the areas mentioned in this work. He currently resides in Tulsa, Oklahoma, with his wife, Arla.